FARM LIFE II
LAKELAND Dales

No dye is necessary to tinge their wool...
Sheep and shepherds are clothed alike.

William Gilpin (1772)

Waving his hat, the shepherd, from the vale
Directs his winding dog the cliffs to scale –
The dog, loud barking, 'mid the glittering rocks,
Hunts, where his master points, the intercepted flocks.

William Wordsworth, in *An Evening Walk*

FARM LIFE IN THE LAKELAND DALES

by

W R Mitchell

DalesCountry

For
Sue and Ivan Godfrey

A **DalesCountry** Book.

First published in the United Kingdom in 2005.

Copyright © W R Mitchell 2005.

The moral right of the author has been asserted.

ISBN 0 946184 62 3

Typeset in Sabon, printed and bound in the United Kingdom
by Lamberts Print & Design, Station Road, Settle,
North Yorkshire, BD24 9AA

Published by DalesCountry, Watershed Mill, Settle,
North Yorkshire, BD24 9LR.

Contents

Illustrations

Cover paintings – E Jeffrey.
Photographs by the author.
Line drawings by E Jeffrey, Frank Sanderson and Alec Wright.

Eskdale 63

Setting the Scene...

The Lake District, in the county of Cumbria, is small in the European context. As the crow flies, the distance from Ennerdale in the west to Shap in the east is forty miles, which an energetic person might walk in 24 hours. Yet here is a region of infinite variety – a rugged dome, with a radial drainage pattern created when old river valleys and fault lines were eroded and smoothed by glacial action.

Closely associated with Lakeland, from the Bronze Age to the present day, are herdwick sheep – a hardy, agile, coarse-fleeced breed well suited to dining on the scanty herbage of the central and western fells. Each herdwick is *heafed*, forming a strong attachment to its natal area – to the spot where it drank in its mother's milk. Disturb a herdwick and it might give you a sneeze of disapproval. Or just stand, regarding you with eyes as ancient-looking as the rocks until it is lost to sight in mist.

A herdwick was said to eat anything green, including holly, ivy and moss from the rocks and walls. Herdwick Billy, one of the old-time characters, told me of a sheep that was wrapped in snow for twenty-one days and lived to bleat the tale. The only time Billy had been "pushed" to fodder herdwicks was in 1917, when he was living at Watendlath. "It's a real high-lying place; we had a lot of winter that year." A herdwick would "stand a fair amount of weather." Thus spake my old friend Joseph Gregg, who farmed in Great Langdale, where up to 100 inches of rain a year fell and the fells might be layered by snow and ice for weeks on end. One of the herdwick's consolations, said Joe, was that under its "jacket" of coarse wool was a "waistcoat" of finer wool.

Discount the fanciful claim that the initial stock of herd-wicks was washed ashore near St Bees from a wrecked galleon of the Spanish Armada. Think instead of the improvement of a rough old breed by selective breeding. It received a boost and a name in monastic times. "Herdwyck" was originally applied to a sheep farm belonging to Furness Abbey, whose primary interest was in the wool, some of which was shipped from Piel Island in Morecambe Bay to the Continent.

The little herdwick became bound to the landscape – to dales lying at around or a little above sea level and to fells rising sheer to tickle the clouds at over 2,000 ft. On the heights, there were few walls. The tenant of a farm accepted a specific number of sheep, selling the wool and the surplus stock. When he gave up the tenancy, he left at the farm the same number of animals in a similar condition. And so the *heaf*-going instinct was preserved. My interest in the farm life of the Lakeland dales began in the Springtime of 1951 when I became Editor of the magazine *Cumbria*, a name not yet adopted for the county. I held the job for nearly forty years. Venturing into the dales, I recorded the dialect-laden memories of extraordinary people in the last phase of a traditional way of life that had served the area for centuries.

I joined the farmers at the Shepherds' Meets, Merry Neets and the fairs at which herdwick tips [tups] were leased for the year for one or two pounds, served the yows [ewes] and were returned to their owners at a fair in spring. By such means was the vital "change of blood" achieved. I wrote a radio script about John Peel, huntsman, for local radio when Carlisle was merely an outpost of BBC Newcastle and in the Civic Hall at Carlisle heard the Men of the Fells record a lusty rendering of the song. I avoided, as did Alexander Craig Gibson, an idealised farmer portrayed by visiting writers and poets. Gibson, writing in the nineteenth century, preferred to think of a Lakeland dalesman as "a rugged down-to-earth sort of figure."

Such was Herdwick Billy, who immortalised his favourite herdwick tup in stained glass at his home near the outflow of Bassenthwaite Lake. I heard from him old customs in the herdwick country, such as the use of cloths known as *twinter clouts* that were attached to young sheep to prevent them being mated. It was a cheap form of birth control for after use the cloths were washed and put away for use in the next mating season. I experienced dalehead hospitality from the Naylors of Wasdale Head and from the Edmondsons of Seathwaite, in their own little valley at the head of Borrowdale. Peggy Ellwood, working in the big old kitchen of Wallabarrow, in the Duddon Valley, spoke entertainingly about the old days, such as when twins were born at a remote farm without the intervention of doctor or midwife. In the absence of piped water, the new-born were cleaned up using water straight from t'beck.

I met Tom Storey, shepherd to Mrs Heelis, better known as Beatrix Potter (1866-1943), who wrote enchanting books about rabbits and other little creatures wearing clothes and having adventurous lives. A Londoner whose introduction to the Lake District came through long summer holidays at prime spots in the area, she used income from royalties from the sale of her book about Peter Rabbit to buy Hill Top, a farm at Near Sawrey. This enabled her periodically to break away from what had been a rigid family circle.

Beatrix's interest in Lakeland farming became focussed on the herdwick breed of sheep. Having appointed Tom Storey to rear animals of good quality, she took great pride in attending Lakeland shows, drawing attention to her stock, though – according to Tom – not always identifying the right pen of sheep. She bought a stake in Lakeland through the purchase of land and more stock. In 1913, aged 47, she married her solicitor, William Heelis (1871-1945) and they lived at Castle Cottage. Hill Top was henceforth a place to which she resorted to sketch or paint. It also became a repository for her valuables.

For the next three decades, Beatrix enlarged her stake in the Lake District, anxious that the life and traditions she first knew and enjoyed should endure as far as possible. She bought farms, mostly those at the dalehead, together with their stocks of herdwick sheep. She was associated with the breeders' association. Where land was under consideration by builders, she acquired it. A family friendship with Canon H D Rawnsley, one of the founders of The National Trust, led to her working closely with this conservation body. In 1930, when buying the Monk Coniston estate of 5,000 acres, she had arranged that the National Trust would purchase half of it from her when the money had been raised. For six years, she managed the estate which was part of a generous bequest in her will. Her husband would receive all. On his death, the National Trust inherited 15 farms and over 4,000 acres of land.

Sixty years ago, I met cycling farmers, walking postmen and blacksmiths shoeing horses in a pre-haytime rush of work. There was a clear division between men's and women's work. The Lakeland farmer liked to think of himself as t'boss, though it was his wife – the most dynamic of the duo – who held the family and the farm together. I met farmers who, from the clothing point of view, looked alike. Their working garb consisted of a flat tweed cap, a Union shirt made of heavy cotton with a neck-band but no collar, and knee-breeches worn in conjunction with leather gaiters or ankle-straps. A waistcoat was worn, the pockets of which held a watch that had been handed down in the family, some *bacca* [tobacco] for smoking or chewing and mints, the flavour of which off-set the earthy farm tang. Many farmers donned a *kitle*, which was a light, hard-wearing coat of durable fabric. They hand-milked their few cows while sitting on three-legged stools.

On the domestic front, women did the washing, baking and the churning that converted cream from the week's milking into saleable butter. Sidney Cole, of Brownrigg, a farm on the 1,000 ft contour near Caldbeck, recalled when Andrew Scott mowed a three and a-half acre field with a scythe. At harvest time, sheaves were hand-tied. People clattered about in clogs.

Brownrigg carried a small quantity of stock. "You were thought to be in a big way if you had 25 cows and six or eight calves." In autumn, surplus stock was sold at the auction marts. The *hoggs* [young sheep] were driven from farms in the high dale country to winter grazings on the marshes of Morecambe Bay or Solway.

Farming in the upper dales evolved as a response to a rocky terrain, to a grey, weepy climate and to a long, long winter. Lakeland has no permanent snow cover, but there may be snow powdering the "tops", over 2,500 ft, on a hundred days of the year. Snow might fall as early as September and linger as late as June. Wordsworth loved those "bold bursts of sunshine, the descending vapours, wandering lights and shadows and the invigorating torrents and waterfalls with which broken weather, in a mountainous region, is accompanied." Canon Rawnsley claimed that spring and autumn were the best times of the year. Percy Withers, who lived near Derwentwater, summed up the Lakeland climate briefly in 1914, observing: "Cloud, wind, rain! – there is not a month of the twelve on which we can count on anything different." In that same year, Nancy Price advised caution when mist was driving, having heard from a local man: "Ah've learnt t' fear 'im, 'e can drive t'sun oot o' tha life as easy as off t'fellside. Ah lost ma boy through 'im yance an' 'e tuk ma man eears agone. Aye, 'e near oalas forgits ta send 'em back."

There was an element of black-magic. Cattle affected by a debilitating ailment known as *murrain* were fumigated – driven through the dense smoke from the *needfire* that received a coverlet of green leaves. Harriet Martineau, a Victorian writer living at Ambleside, heard of a farmer who, having treated his beasts, sent his ailing wife through the smoke. The last known *needfire* ran its smoky course at Troutbeck in 1851.

Taming the Wilderness

Pollen deposited in peat bogs and on the shores of lakes reveals that a process of denudation began in the Neolithic period. A decrease in the amount of tree pollens was matched by an increase in grass pollens. Clearings were being made in which to pasture stock. The first people had arrived in the wake of retreating ice, some 5,000 years ago. They hunted for food with stone-tipped arrows, fished in the lakes and tarns, kept a few cattle and clothed themselves in cured animal skins. Trees – oak, elm and pine – were cleared to provide open ground for crops. The head of an axe was formed from a piece of volcanic tuff wrenched from an outcrop high on Stickle Pike, at the head of Great Langdale, roughly shaped *in situ* with hammers fashioned from pieces of granite and finished off at some temperate coastal site. The Great Cumbrian axe was widely traded.

Neolithic folk clothed themselves in wool, cultivated crops, domesticated animals and made pottery. In the early Bronze Age, the mild climate encouraged the cultivation of some upland areas in the west. As the Bronze Age waned, and the climate became colder and wetter, high fell settlements were abandoned and people and their stock moved to lower ground. Iron Age technology slowly replaced that relating to bronze. The guzzling of restless livestock – sheep, goats, pigs – inhibited the natural regeneration of timber, though by and large the fellsides were left well wooded. Rollinson, reviewing the history of man in the Lake District, believed that the native Cumbrians in pre-Roman times were essentially a hybrid group having characteristics that belonged to the Neolithic as well as the Bronze Age.

As this hybrid culture advanced, it became customary for the dead to be cremated and the remains placed in urns. It is deduced from the remains of settlements such as Ewe Close, near Crosby Ravensworth, that a tribal centre was a village with hut circles and stone-fenced fields and that scattered around were a relatively large number of single farms. Grain would be cultivated. Sheep and cattle grazed on the hills. Extending along the western seaboard from Scotland to Cornwall was the so-called Celtic fringe, though Celts would not leave their mark as prominently in Lakeland as in other Celtic territories.

A thin scattering of Celtic settlements abut the fells. The Celtic presence is most evident in names given to natural features – to rivers and hills. River names are short, sometimes sharp, including Kent, Leven, Winster, Irt and Esk. Celts named Skiddaw, Blencathra, Helvellyn and Maiden Moor, the "maiden" derived from *myddyn*, meaning middle. Penrith and Penruddock incorporate the Celtic *pen*, for head, and in Glencoyne is the Celtic *glyn* for valley. Before the arrival of the Romans, a sub-group of the Brigantean tribe occupied those parts of the Lake District that were habitable. The Celts were influential before Roman times. Their endurance occasionally flared into hostility towards the conquering force. When the Roman legions departed, four hundred years later, the Celtic influence was evident from the fifth to the eighth centuries.

Sheep-counting numerals are a curious survival from Celtic times. A popular form begins: *Yan, Tan, Tethra, Methra, Pip...* Each word probably represented a group of five rather than a single sheep. At Coniston, shepherds counted thus: 1 Yan, 2 taen, 3 tedderte, 4 meddderte, 5 pimp, 6, sethra, 7 lethera, 8 hovera, 9 dovera, 10 dik, 11 Yan-a-dik, 12 taen-a-dik, 13 tedder-a-dik, 14 medder-a-dik, 15 mimpth, 16 Yan-a-mimph, 17 taen-a-mimph, 18 tedder-a-mimph, 19 medder-a-mimph, 20 giggot.

In the seventh century, the Anglians, an agricultural people – and the first English – invaded the Lake District from Northumbria in the east and penetrated some way up the main valleys. A people more concerned with crops than sheep would find the dale-country unappealing. In gentler country, using heavy ox-drawn ploughs, they cultivated the heavy land that had frustrated earlier farmers. So the scattering of Celtic folk was by and large left undisturbed – until the arrival of the Norse-Irish settlers. These were land-hungry Norsemen from Scandinavia. At a time when the climate was mild, they voyaged in open boats to Iceland and Greenland. Others rounded Cape Wrath ("the turning point"), some to settle in Ireland and, by about the year 850, in the Isle of Man. They inter-married with the local Celts.

The Norse expansion continued in the late ninth and tenth centuries when groups beached their longboats beside the Duddon and other estuaries. From coastal settlements, they ventured into the farmless upper dales, doubtless fusing with any dark-haired Celts they encountered. The progress of the colonisation was surprisingly rapid, judging by changes to the vegetation, from oakwood to open grazing. Norse settlers did not live up to the popular image of warlike invaders, keen to rob, to burn, to kill. This was not a belligerent force as in the case of the invasion of Danes along the East Coast. They came as settlers, pastoralists, greedy for new land. They kept sheep, cattle, pigs and goats. They controlled grazing on the hills through *stints*, each *stint* relating to the pasturage of a domestic animal. The rate of stockage for other livestock was assessed according to their size and appetite. An area of about eight acres was known as a *grass*.

Many of the settlers became Christian, as evidenced by wheel-head crosses and hogback tombs at places of worship on lower ground. Documentary evidence of the Scandinavian settlement is sparse. Yet Norse terms would become the language of topography, examples being *tjorn, fjall, bekkr* and *dalr* for tarn, fell, beck and dale respectively. Scafell is a name derived from the Old Norse *skalli*, meaning bald. Crinkle Crags, at the head of Great Langdale, is from the Norse

14

kringla, meaning a circle. Near their homesteads were small patches of arable land, as at Rydal (where rye was grown) and Haverthwaite (oats). The dialect of Cumbrian folk would preserve many names from Old Norse, examples being *brant* for steep and *slape* for slippery. Rushes were known as *seaves*.

W G Collingwood, historian, compared the Norse settlement of Lakeland with that of Iceland, as noted in the *Landnamobok*. A farm would be established at the mouth of a dale. Woodland would be cleared to form a *thwaite*. In due course, scores of *thwaites* with their attendant buildings were created. In High Furness, an echo of Norse times is detected in a litany of attractive names – Satterthwaite, Graythwaite, Finsthwaite and Haverthwaite. In the north are Crosthwaite, Braithwaite, Rosthwaite and Thornthwaite, each named after some prominent local feature. Further up the dales were *booths*, temporary huts that in due course became sites of permanent settlement. The booth of Ulfkell, at the head of Eskdale, was in stages to take on the curious name of Brotherilkeld.

As in Scandinavia, the settlers practised transhumance. In summer, they drove their cattle and sheep from the home farm to areas where they might take advantage of a flush of new grass. A summer pasture was known as a *saeter* or *sheiling*. The sheiling of Amal or Hamal, at the head of Windermere, with other *saeters*, was to evolve into Ambleside. The term *saeter* lives on as an element of Seatoller, at the head of Borrowdale, this name signifying a place among the alder trees. Hawkshead is derived from Haukr's saeter. The word laith, from the Old Norse word *hlaoa*, means a storehouse or barn. Farmsteads of stone and thatch, with attendant crofts, were sited beside fellside becks, which provided a copious supply of fresh water.

Picture, if you will, the summertime occupation of huts, each with a low drystone wall capped by a wigwam-like structure of wood thatched with turf. It is likely that the earthen floor would be strewn with bracken. Cattle in an adjacent enclosure would be regularly milked. Much of the goodness of milk would be locked up in the form of cheese for winter consumption. In the old days, the hilltops and the dales were grazed and the hillsides were left well-wooded, the resort of pigs that in good years laid on fat for the winter by guzzling the acorn crop. Placenames like Grisedale (from *griss*, pig), Grasmere (*griss-mere*) and Swindale (*svina*, meaning swine) perpetuate the ancient association.

In Borrowdale (originally *borgar dalr* – valley of the fort) the Norse detestation of crowds is evident in the generous spacing between the farms and small villages. Few traces of Norse farmsteads have been found. Presumably the sites were so good that stone-built farmsteads supplanted them. Norse terms for sheep include *gimmer* [female] and *twinter* [a two-year-old animal]. A Norse love of sport lives on in Cumberland and Westmorland style wrestling, at which a dale farmer's son – accustomed to handling lively sheep – was especially good. The Norsefolk, though well-spread, were community-minded. At *things*, men gathered to hear proclamations affecting them all. (The Tynwald ceremony endures on the Isle of Man). A terraced mound behind the Fell Foot farm, at the head of Little Langdale, may have been the setting for a *thing*.

Wheel-head stone crosses, bearing pagan as well as Christian symbols, are found mainly at the periphery of the fell country. Old Norse endured as a living language in some of the dales until the 12th century and contributed to a smattering of Cumbrian dialect. Most of the personal names, Christian or surname, post-date the Norman period.

Monastic Farming

From the departure of the Romans to the arrival of the Normans, most of Cumbria was part of an independent British kingdom, sandwiched between Scotland and England, with the border switching from one to another. The Norman invaders regarded it as part of Scotland until, in 1092, William Rufus marched north and took Carlisle from Dolfin, son of Gospatrick. A castle was built to defend the newly-won territory and English settlers were brought in – peasant families and their livestock, described in the *Anglo-Saxon Chronicle* as "...very many country folk, with their wives and their cattle." They were "to dwell there and cultivate the land." The Scots regained Cumbria for Scotland in 1137. In 1157, Malcolm IV of Scotland handed it to Henry II. The alliance along the border was an uneasy one for centuries.

With the coming of the Normans, baronies were created, castles were built at the fringes of the Lake District and, with handsome grants from new landowners, the monastic system flourished, giving stability and a sense of order to the region for well over four centuries. Professor H C Darby commented, with regard to the Anglian and Norse-Irish settlements in Cumbria: "No later invasion of peoples modified the Anglian-Scandinavian pattern, for the Norman Conquest was the transposition of an aristocracy and not a folk movement of new settlers on the land." The written Norse language endured into the twelfth century.

Furness Abbey, by the Bay, had extensive properties on the Silurian hills of southern Lakeland. Furness, founded by the order of Savigny, merged with the Cistercians in 1147. The monastic buildings, in the Vale of the Deadly Nightshade, were on a grand scale, using the local red sandstone, lead and iron from local mines, also timber from the extensive woodlands.

The monks and their guests lived well. The sea and lakes provided them with fish. Char, recovered from the depths of Windermere, was an especial favourite. The larder also held venison from the free-ranging red and roe deer and meat from wild boar that had stuffed themselves on pannage. Furness had meat from sheep and cattle established on rich pastureland.. With the exception of hilly Shap, established by monks of the Premonstratensian Order, the monasteries were outside the Lakeland core. At Shap, oats were grown. Winter grazing for the livestock was ensured through crop rotations. Sheep grazed the hills lying to the east of Ullswater. Surplus livestock, slaughtered in autumn, was salted down for the winter.

Of the peripheral monasteries with land in the central area, St Bees had the title deeds for the manor of Ennerdale and the fells above Loweswater. They also held a right of pannage for swine in the western dales. In a document of 1334 there is reference to "the head of Eynerdale", possibly Gillerthwaite, which then was a cattle ranch known as a vaccary. Gillerthwaite is mentioned in the sixteenth century when its tenants were repeatedly fined for breaches of customs of the manor. One such breach was permitting cattle and sheep to stray on to the forest – the land on which the lord of the manor hunted.

The ruling families, who held sway over much of the Lake District, granted land to their relatives and followers. One of many examples concerned William I de Lancaster. Between 1140 and 1170, he granted to Roger, son of Orm of Kirkby Ireleth, land in Seathwaite and Dunnerdale. Monasteries that had been established for prayerful meditation in wild places were soon creating wealth to bolster their earthly ambitions and the glorification of their buildings. New land was brought into agricultural use. Granted large tracts of fell country, *granges* [abbey farms] were set up and so the fells became more productive. In 1242, a vast tract of upper Eskdale was acquired from David de Mulcaster – a swap involving Monk Foss, one of the abbey's properties at the foot of Black Combe. The deal included Brotherilkeld, a sheep farm running to about 14,000 acres. By 1250, around 1,400 acres in Upper Eskdale had become sheep runs. The area was also noted for the preservation of red deer.

In Borrowdale, most of which had been purchased from Alice de Rumeli, heiress of the Barony of Allerdale, a grange was established on a level site where the River Derwent flowed into Derwentwater. The monastic *Coucher Book* (1396) held a reference to *grangia nostra de Boroudale* – "our grange in Borrowdale". This Furness outlier abutted land that Fountains Abbey had received from the aforementioned Alice. The sway of Fountains was experienced at Watendlath and Langstrath, also Hestholm (now known as Derwent Island, in Derwentwater). For a time, therefore, two great Cistercian abbeys owned a goodly part of the central fells, grazing them with cattle and sheep.

The ownership of the dairy farm of Stonethwaite was the subject of much inter-monastery wrangling. When Edward I confiscated the property in 1304 Fountains purchased it from him for 40s. Furness, keen to increase the number of customary tenants, obtained a licence from the King in 1338 to enclose large tracts of land, which were named *parks*, a term of French origin, introduced at the Conquest to describe ground enclosed for farming, either pastoral or arable. Instances of this were Abbot Park, Stott Park and Oxen Park. Twenty-seven granges listed in Furness included Bouth, Nibthwaite, Oxen Park, Haverthwaite, Graythwaite, Sawrey and Elterwater.

Sheep were kept mainly for their wool, the high quality of which was known throughout Europe. At the beginning of fourteenth century, Furness Abbey was disposing of thirty sacks a year. Packhorses transported wool from Borrowdale over high passes to abbey warehouses by Morecambe Bay, from whence it was exported. The fourteenth century was to be a difficult time for Cumbrians, who had to contend with raids by the Scots. With possessions extending from sea level to the craggy pate of Coniston Old Man (2,635 ft), Furness had a base at Hawkshead for the Furness Fells and the fell country twixt Coniston Water and Windermere. By the 1530s, Hawkshead was worth almost three times as much as Dalton, which was the administrative centre of Low Furness.

Between the 12th and 16th centuries, the deer forest declined as their ancestral lands were used for arable crops or as pasture for cattle. Stocks of sheep, introduced to the waste, grazed in relative safety because predators such as the wolf had been "extirpated". The few remaining eagles, found guilty of taking lambs, had their nests rifled. In 1535, just prior to the Dissolution, when Parliament ordered a survey of the income of religious houses, Furness was found to be drawing income from the rent of "divers granges, fields, meadows, fisheries within the manor." This amounted to an awesome £102.15.8. Livestock named in the survey were cattle, sheep, lambs, hens, geese and capons. Barley, oats and wheat were also listed and butter and cheese were produced. At the Dissolution, Richard Greames of Esk in Netherby purchased from the Crown the estate in Borrowdale that had been owned by Fountains Abbey. Thomas, Lord Wharton leased the manor and demesnes of Shap.

The demise of the great monasteries caused inconvenience or suffering to some but the Lakeland economy did not collapse. Mary C Fair wrote that the sheep presumably went with the granges of the abbeys to the new grantees, who would need shepherds. Trade in such a commodity as wool had passed through the monasteries and was now dealt with at urban markets in such places as Kendal, Ulverston and Cockermouth. Lakeland wool, being coarse, did not claim the best of prices. Cumbria, with its small, compact agricultural settlements, operated within the framework of a feudal system. C M L Bouch and G P Jones, in *The Lake Counties 1500-1830* wrote: "A traveller in Tudor times would have seen small villages and hamlets, each surrounded by a few fields of culti-vated land, with common adjoining and then a waste stretching for miles until the next oasis of cultivation was reached and crossed, if at all, by road and often hardly pass-able tracks." The pastoral qualities were off-set by traces of industry. In the woods, smoke rose from *bloomeries*, where iron ore was being smelted using charcoal as a fuel. Slag heaps testified to the places where copper, lead and silver were being mined. At the head of Borrowdale was a closely-guarded mine from which came *wad* [plumbago, also known as black lead].

Men of Property

Celia Fiennes, a visitor to "these Northern Countyes" in 1695, reported "noe wheat or Rhye for they are so cold and Late in their yeare they Cannot venture at that sort of tillage." Away from the hills, a greater variety of crops might be found. Celia, travelling on horseback between Windermere and Ullswater, saw "villages of sad little hutts made up of drye walls, only stones piled together and the roofs of same slatt." There seemed to be "little or no tunnells for their chimneys and have no morter or plaister within or without." She took them at first to be outbuildings in which cattle were foddered, "not thinking them to be dwelling houses." All that Celia found to appease her hunger was "clap bread and butter and cheese and a cup of beer."

The dalesfolk were not entirely cut off from the outer world. Goods and gossip travelled with the packhorse trains that followed a network of tracks for centuries until the transport revolution of the early nineteenth century. By 1770, packhorses linked the main towns, from Whitehaven to Kendal, which as an important trading centre for wool was especially busy. It was estimated that no less than 230 packhorses were regularly using the town each week. Packhorse bridges, spanning becks and gorges like rainbows set in stone, came into being between 1660 and 1760. In the late nineteenth century, when railways were well established, the packhorse route from Kendal to Whitehaven was still used in the traditional sense, with laden horses crossing the high passes of Wrynose and Hardknott.

In the dale-country, where the growing season for crops was short, a variety of oats known as *skegg* was favoured. Some *bigg* [a substitute for barley] was grown. In 1766, a Cumberland writer in the *Gentleman's Magazine* reported that "land is kept so cold and spongy that we cannot sow oats before April and *bigg* before June." The wet and frost in winter was very unfavourable for wheat. "Our lands, with the vast quantity of manure we must employ... costs one third at least more to till than yours [in the south], and does not produce half the crops yours produces." He noted that "the middle of February is the middle of our winter and the farmers must have one half of their straw, and two thirds of their hay at that time, or their stock perishes. We cannot turn out our horses and cows to grass till the beginning of June..." Arthur Young (1771), viewing the landscape between Keswick and Penrith, saw "much of it moors and quite uncultivated, though evidently capable of it". Between Shap and Kendal was "a continuous chain of mountainous moors, totally uncultivated." The farmers grew a few turnips, knew little of clover.

Monarch of the Dale was the herdwick tup. The sheep foraged on the fells for most of the year, each stock tending to keep to its own ground. If straying did occur, a sheep was readily identifiable from a clipping of its *lugs* [ears], from horn burns and from markings on the fleece which were renewed annually at clipping time. Durable marks on wool were made using red iron oxide, known to the dale farmers as *ruddle*. Herdwicks were weatherwise, though a sudden blizzard might overblow a number of them. Snowblown sheep might live for a week or two in their snow-caves providing there was an air hole. They nibbled at whatever lay underfoot and in extremism sucked their wool. The old-time flock of herdwicks was small, around fifty animals. The wool clip, though not of especially good quality, formed the basis of the Lakeland woollen industry. Surplus cattle were slaughtered in autumn and the meat salted, then cut into *collops*, to be hung in the big chimneys to dry. Only the milk cattle, a bull and oxen used for work were over-wintered. Horse-drawn sleds transported hay and bracken across *brant* [steep] hillsides.

In what would become known as the Romantic Age (c1760-

1840), the dale country was opened up to tourism. Visitors were captivated when they encountered a self-sufficient farmer following a quaint pastoral routine. The Yeomen of Lakeland, known fancifully to some as *statesmen*, held their land by customary tenure rather than by copyhold, with the stipulation that they would take up arms in any Border warfare. Through an agreement reached with Elizabeth I in 1586 they might hand on their estate at death to their next of kin. With an end to the Border troubles, an effort was made to take away the old rights of tenure. A flurry of lawsuits and petitions led to a decision of the King's Bench in 1625 that upheld the tenants' rights.

So there came into being a new landed class who, with security of tenure, set about improving their holdings. The increasing value of wool, cattle and timber put money in their pockets. William Hutchinson (1794) described them as "people of property" who had "received a tolerable education and have been somewhat from home." Wordsworth's grand style of prose about the *statesmen* was worthy of being set to music: "Towards the head of these Dales was found a perfect Republic of Shepherds and Agriculturalists, among whom the plough of each man was confined to the maintenance of his own family or to the occasional accommodation of his neighbour. Two or three cows furnished each family with milk and cheese...Neither high-born nobleman, knight nor esquire was here; but many of these humble sons of the hills had a consciousness that the land, which they walked over and tilled, had for more than five hundred years been possessed by men of their name and blood..."

W G Collingwood (1925) sniffed at the use of *statesman*. Men who owned their estates, however small, or held them with special fixity of tenure, were more properly described as yeomen. Indeed. The term *statesman* did not appear in printed form until the later years of the 18th century. Dr Charles Moor, poring over parish registers for northern parts, seldom encountered the term, though "yeoman" appeared with great frequency. Mary C Fair, in a letter to the magazine *Cumbria*, described *statesman* as a colloquial term of comparatively recent origin. "The term is never used in legal or official documents, yeoman being always so employed. Romantic-minded writers of later times seem to have adopted the use of the colloquial statesmen instead of yeomen for our local farmers..."

J D Marshall drew together the published research and propounded his own ideas in a paper entitled *"Statesmen" in Cumbria: the Vicissitudes of an Expression*, published in the Transactions of the Cumberland & Westmorland Antiquarian & Archaeological Society. Marshall noted that where parish registers and other types of local list referred to land-occupiers, they almost invariably use the terms yeoman or husbandman. A farmer was referred to as such towards the end of the 18th century. In the parish records of Furness, the use of statesman before 1803 was slight – an entry at Ulverston in that year relating to "Thomas Towers, Statesman", buried on 6 January, aged 81. Further examples followed in 1805 and 1807. The comparative slowness in assuming both written and printed forms in Cumbria suggested to Marshall that the word was an importation. It was inclined to be adopted by some members of the yeomanry as they began to climb the social scale, becoming increasingly status-conscious, and by others who felt their status was being threatened.

Statesmen, a provincialism known in the south-east of England, had little fashionable association of a romantic kind before the very end of the 18th century. From being recognised by a few constables in a few Westmorland villages, the *statesmen* became central features of the Cumbrian scene, popularised through the writings of Wordsworth and John Houseman. It seemed strange to Marshall that it should have been necessary to import a word used in Surrey, Sussex or East Anglia in order to give a Cumbrian yeoman the sense of pride that he already had a means of expressing.

When Thomas Williamson, a yeoman, of Common, in the township of Applethwaite, died in 1735, an inventory of his goods noted: Husbandry Gear and a Garner, £2.10.0; Live Stock Beasts and a Horse, £16.5.0; Sheep Young and Old, £12.0.0; Pultery etc, 2s.6; Stocks of Hay and Straw, Bigg and Oats, £7.0.0; Meal, Malt and Household Provisions, £1.10.0. During the 18th century, the numbers of yeomen declined. Changes in agricultural practices strengthened landowners at the expense of freeholders. The rich got richer, the poor poorer. The enclosures of the common land and the fell slopes deprived many villagers of long-held rights, making them dependent on the landowners. Many of the yeomen farmers could not afford to equip their holdings for the new husbandry. Their numbers halved between 1770 and 1820.

Some yeomen, like the Patricksons of Ennerdale, the Sandys of Graythwaite and the Fletchers of Wasdale, sprang from this frugal but self-sufficient freeholding class to become gentlemen. The Patricksons had a coat-of-arms as early as 1592. One of the Sandys families, having petitioned James I, obtained a market charter for Hawkshead. The Fletchers achieved a baronetcy in 1640. Generations of the Browne family, living at Townhead, Troutbeck, achieved social distinction when, in 1667, George held the office of High Constable of Kendal Ward. Though never granted the right to display arms, the Brownes had bogus arms carved on a fine *court cupboard* set in a wall of their home.

William Pearson (1780-1856), the son of a yeoman farmer, of Yews, Crosthwaite, at the head of the Lyth Valley, became a much-respected friend of William Wordsworth when the poet was living at Rydal Mount. Less fortunate Lakeland families, foundering during the social turmoil of the 18th century, became labourers, yet social differences between farmer and worker remained slight –

And o'fare't alike – beath maister and man

In eatin' and drinkin' or wark;
They turn'd out at morn and togidder began
And left off togidder at dark.

Harriet Martineau commented on the decline of the yeomen in 1855. The "first great change" had been from the opening of carriage-roads. "There was the temptation then to carry stock and grain to fairs and markets. More grain was grown than the household needed, and offered for sale. In a little while, the mountain-farmers were sure to fail in competition in the markets with dwellers in agricultural districts. The mountaineer had no agricultural science and little skill; and the decline of the fortunes of the 'statesmen'... has been regular and mournful to witness. They haunt the fairs and markets, losing in proportion to the advance of improvement elsewhere."

On their first losses, they began to mortgage their lands. "After bearing the burden of these mortgages till they could bear it no longer, their children have sold the lands...The farmer was tempted to lose the remembrance of his losses in drink when he attended the fairs and markets."

Yeomen at Home

A long-house plan saw men and animals living under the same roof-tree. Towards the end of the 17th century, when recovery was well in hand after the setback caused by the Civil War, the ambition of many yeomen was to have a house made of stone. A writer in *Gentleman's Magazine* (1790), referring in particular to the southern part of Cumberland, observed: "The rust of poverty and ignorance is gradually wearing off... the houses (or rather huts) of clay, which were small and ill-built, are mostly thrown down; instead of which strong and roomy farmhouses are built... with hard durable stone, which is very plentiful here." What Professor W G Hoskins was to call a "Great Re-building in Stone" led to the adoption of a standard pattern. R W Brunskill, an authority on vernacular architecture, dubbed this the "statesman plan". A stone and slate farmhouse was based on a medieval concept that in turn sprang from the ancient long-house. The size of the new type of house depended on the wealth of its builder.

Basically it consisted of a single range of farm buildings and a dwelling house, separated by a hallan, or cross passage. This extended from the *mell* [front door] to the back door, between the *down house* [service area] where washing and brewing took place and the *fire house* [living accommodation]. The most conspicuous feature of the living room was an immense inglenook, with a *runnel balk* [beam] from which mutton hams were suspended to smoke. Commodities like salt, which must be kept dry, were placed in a *spice cupboard* in a recess adjacent to the fireplace. The main bedrooms were on the second storey. Children and servants slept in a loft, access to which was by wooden ladder. The loft was devoid of a ceiling, being open to the slates and rafters.

In his history of Hawkshead, Cowper believed that in some cases the foundations of the new house were sketched out a few yards from the old farm. After its abandonment, the medieval farmstead might be converted into a barn. This variation of the "statesman plan" involved the separation of the byre and barn from the house. There came into use, between about 1650 and 1750, a type of house with a long, low roofline. A circular chimney was the best use of rubble Usually there were no windows in the gable-end. Family pride was reflected in the initials and date carved into stone above the main entrance. Within the house, a similar claim to ownership was carved on heavy furnishings such as the oaken bread or court cupboards built into the wooden partition between kitchen and *bower* [best bedroom]. Such a cupboard was often used to store the unleavened *haver bread*. Flagstones were widely used for covering an earthen floor.

Townend at Troutbeck, near Windermere, is an early example of a successful yeoman's home. George Browne built it between 1623 and 1626 for his bride Susan Rawlinson, of Grisedale Hall, Lancashire. (The house was to be the Browne family home until 1944). Larger than others of its kind, Townend had the addition of two wings with numerous chimneys of the circular style. A massive oak staircase led to the bedrooms. Glencoyne Farm, Patterdale, another fine example of a yeoman's home, situated beside a beck that was the boundary between Westmorland and Cumberland, has crow-stepped gables and tall cylindrical chimneys. The oldest part of Hartsop Hall, near the head of Patterdale, was built in the fifteenth century, having walls a yard thick. Mullioned windows and fine oak beams in two the rooms testify to its antiquity. A coat of arms on the staircase signifies that the property once belonged to the Lancasters. In common with many old houses, Hartsop Hall has several sycamore trees growing near it. Formerly such trees provided good perches for cuckoos. They were also said to act as lightning conductors.

Wordsworth considered the village of Hartsop as being "remarkable for its cottage architecture." Here are several properties with so-called *spinning galleries*, mostly dating from the sixteenth and seventeenth centuries. Narrow, built of timber, quite often on the north side of a barn, they overhung the ground and were approached by an outside staircase. These were hardly the conditions under which a spinster would feel comfortable. Was the so-called *spinning gallery* a means of providing access to the upper part of an outbuilding without impinging on the main space? Or used for drying damp wool before it was stored away to await collection? If spinsters spun here, it would doubtless be for a time just after sheep-clipping, which usually was the brightest, warmest time of the year.

An outstanding example of a barn with a ramp leading to the upper floor – a structure designed to occupy a steep slope – exists at Townend, Troutbeck. Above one of the doors is a carved stone: G E B 1666. This type of barn, rare in Britain, is nonetheless common in Norway. Cattle occupied the lower floor. The ramp gave access to the mewstead, where hay was stored. (At Troutbeck, in addition to these features, there are two wings, built possibly to accommodate labourers on the Browne farm).

Thomas Gray, touring Lakeland in late September, 1769, entered the Vale of Grasmere, an "unsuspected paradise". All was "peace, rusticity and happy poverty, in its neatest, most becoming attire." Here were "hanging inclosures, corn fields and meadows, green as an emerald, with their trees and hedges, and cattle, fill up the whole space from the edge of the water." A large farmhouse at the bottom of a steep smooth lawn was "embosomed in old woods, which climb half way up the mountain's side..."

Gray's Journal gives us a tourist's vivid impression of Borrowdale in the eighteenth century. He met "a civil young farmer overseeing his reapers (for it is oat-harvest here) who conducted us to a neat white house in the village of Grange, which is built on a rising ground the midst of a valley... For me I went no further than the farmer's (better than four miles from Keswick) at Grange." Access beyond Seathwaite was "barred to prying mortals, only there is a little path winding over the Fells, and for some weeks in the year passable to the Dale's-men; but the mountains know well that these innocent people will not reveal the mysteries of their ancient kingdom." The dreadful road, he was told, dividing again, "leads one branch to *Ravenglass* and the other to *Hawkshead.*"

The farmer he encountered near Grange had in the previous year plundered the eyrie of golden eagles. "All the dale are up in arms on such an occasion, for they lost abundance of lambs yearly, not to mention hares, partridges, grouse, etc." The farmer was let down from the cliff in ropes, reaching the shelf of the rock on which the nest was built, "the people above shouting and hallooing to fright the old birds, which flew screaming around but did not dare to attack him. He brought off the eaglet (for there is rarely more than one) and an addle egg. The nest was roundish and more than a yard over, made of twigs twisted together. Seldom a year passes, but they take the brood, or eggs, and sometimes they shoot one, sometimes the other, parent; but the survivor has always found a mate (probably in Ireland) and they breed near the old place."

Another Eagle Crag was situated on the almost inaccessible Burtness or Birkness Combe, in neighbouring Buttermere. The eagles dined on lambs belonging to the great sheep farm of Gatesgarth. This enraged one John Vicars who, though a Borrowdale man, helped his father Matthias in managing the farm. An anti-eagle campaign, waged towards the end if the eighteenth century, was described in *Green's New Guide* (1819). Vicars, with great daring, twice removed eaglets from the nest. He attempted to shoot the adults. Eventually, lying in ambush near the head of the lake, he had both birds in line, wounding both of them with one shot. They managed to escape but were picked up dead, one body reposing at

Gillerthwaite and the other at Lamplugh.

In his novel *Thorston Hall*, O S Macdonell gave an imaginative account of the life of a Lakeland farmer during the closing years of the eighteenth century. The fictitious Robert Thorston lived and thought much as his father had done before him. He seldom left the farm and had but few ideas unconnected with it. He occasionally visited the market town of Cockermouth and once a year he travelled nine miles to Keswick to attend the sheep fair. Twice in his life he had been to Whitehaven. Every summer, he and his family spent part of a day with relations at Buttermere, which lay seven miles from home. He knew the limits of his world and had no desire to go further.

Almost everything eaten by such yeoman stock was produced locally. They clothed themselves with wool taken from the backs of the herdwick sheep, spun, woven and made up into garments in the home district. The cloth was hodden grey, being undyed wool, a mix of that from black sheep and white sheep. Many people slept in homespun, woollen nightshirts. Shirts and *brats* [aprons] were made from a cloth fashioned from hemp and flax. Hides, tanned locally, were fashioned by the cobbler into clogs, shoes and gaiters. Only affluent yeoman farmers owned leather saddles. Much more commonplace were green sods, girthed onto the horse with hay bands. Farmers, their wives or daughters, were content with this arrangement. Rabbit skins were cured for hats and bonnets.

In winter, a rush dipped in mutton-fat provided the indoor lighting, giving out a small yellow flame and much smoke. Spices, kept in a cupboard near the fire, were there to impart flavour to a monotonous diet. Oatmeal was in the form of *crowdy* [porridge, known widely as poddish]. Celia Fiennes watched clap bread being baked in the Kendal area about 1695: "They mix their flour with water so soft as to roll it in their hands into a ball – they have a board made round – this is to cast out the cake thinn – as thinn as a paper and still they clap it and drive it round, and then they have a plaite of iron – and so shove off the cake on it and so set it on coales and bake it." Potatoes were not common in the Lake District until the last years of the seventeenth century.

William Gilpin, visiting Rosthwaite in Borrowdale in 1772, saw farmers who had "scanty patches of arable land." They cultivated them with difficulty and their crops, ripening late, and "often a prey to autumnal rains which are violent in this country" just gave them bread to eat. "The herds afford them milk and their flocks cloaths, the shepherd himself being often the manufacturer also." No dye was necessary to tinge their wool, it being naturally a russet brown "and sheep and shepherds are clothed alike." In steep-sided Borrowdale, peat cut on the fells was bundled and fastened on sledges "on each of which a man sits and guides the machine with his foot down the precipice."

Sir Frederick Eden, who died in 1809, described the Cumberland labourer of Georgian times thus: "He wore a hat, a cloth coat and waistcoat, a pair of leathern breeches, although they sometimes wore breeches of flannel or coloured cloth, a linen shirt, stocks and shoes. The women wore a black stuff hat, a linen bedgown, stamped with blue and home-made, a cotton or linen neckcloth, two flannel petticoats, the upper one dyed blue, coarse home-made woollen stockings and a linen shift. They generally wore stays or rather a bodice, and occasionally woollen gowns. On Sundays they wore black silk hats and cotton gowns."

At large farms where grain was threshed, the thwack of a flail might be heard. This consisted of a *swingle* of holly wood, attached by a thong to a long pole made of ash. The *swingle*, brought down flat, was used to separate the grain from the husks. Harriet Martineau (1861) obtained a labourer from an agricultural county "as spade husbandry was a thing unheard-of in my own neighbourhood [Ambleside]. He brought his wife; and his wages were at first 12s a week, out of which he paid the low rent of ls.6d per week for his cottage; a model cottage which I built, with a cow-house adjoining, for £130. These stone dwellings last for ever, and need few or no repairs, so that money is well invested in them."

Hand-knitting of stockings, mittens and other useful items, provided a useful addition to the family income. It was the occupation of men, women and children. Women might knit in one of their homes with the faint light of a peat fire to provide illumination. They rocked and wailed, their songs being related to the number of stitches made. A dagger-like knitting-stick, stuck behind a leather belt, held an extra needle.

Head of Swindale

Enclosing the Land

The boundaries of properties were initially defined by reference to conspicuous natural objects. Then some ditches were made. A ditch excavated at Grasmere in 1279 prevented cattle from trespassing in the deer forest of Rydal. In the following decade, the monks of Furness Abbey were allowed to enclose some thirty acres of sheep pasture at the head of Eskdale with a "dyke, wall or paling" such as the deer of the adjoining forest of Egremont could leap. This boundary marker was constructed of earth and stone. The bounds of the manor of Coniston were defined in part by a hedge "which parts the several Allans belonging to Yewdale from Furness Fell grounds." Hedges were also used in Ennerdale and Langdale.

The process of emparking the land was evident early in the sixteenth century, when Abbot Bank of Furness Abbey created a deer park "about 5 miles compass" at Grizedale. He doubtless wished to provide guests with hunting and was keen to have a reliable source of venison for the abbey. In 1551, a wall was built along the side of Red Screes to distinguish the boundary between the townships of Ambleside and Troutbeck. Elsewhere, by 1537, ten parks lay within the area of the Furness Fells, these probably being established as sheep-runs. During that same century, monastic tenants were undertaking private enclosure on a small scale. Their enclosures were known as *grounds*, the name of each bearing that of the family who reclaimed the land. H S Cowper, author of a history of Hawkshead, found thirty-six *grounds* in Furness alone.

Yeoman farmers at Hawkshead took in new pastureland on Claife Heights, west of Windermere. The names they gave for the enclosures included Waterson Intake, Rough Hows Intake and Moss Eccles Intake. On the higher hillsides were common pastures, used in the spring and clear of stock in the autumn. The stock was wintered on the inbye land.

Thomas West, in his *Antiquities of Furness*, complained that in 1773 "one general obstacle to improvement and advancement of agriculture in Furness is the mixed lands or township fields." Domestic economy called for the improvement of every acre. "This can never be done where there is common pasture, by which every man has it in his power to prevent his neighbour's industry."

Wordsworth's description of a farming community among the fells mentioned "statesmen-farms", the occupiers of which shared a common patch of land sown with arable crops or cultivated as meadows. On the common field, "the several portions" were marked out by "stones, bushes or trees: which portions, where the custom has survived, to this day are called *dales*... to distribute." The valley might lie open but "enclosures seem to have taken place upon the sides of the mountains; because the land there was not intermixed, and was of little comparative value."

Wasdale Head was enclosed in early times, possibly in the seventeenth century, judging by the irregular wall pattern in the valley, which is in marked contrast with the rectangular, eighteenth century enclosures of the fellsides. Such enclosures were called *intakes*, the land having been "taken in". In the reclaimed area, cutting artificial channels drained the land and the soil was sweetened by being overspread with lime. From the mid-eighteenth century until about 1850, vast areas of Lakeland fell country was enclosed within drystone walls. In the late 1700s, the cost of constructing a drystone wall to a height of five and a half feet high was between a 1s.6d and 1s.8d a rood (seven and a-half yards). The process of enclosure was speeded up early in the nineteenth century when the Napoleonic Wars led to a high price for food and wool. The General Enclosure Act of 1801 further stimulated the process. With the rapid growth of industry, a vast urban population must be fed.

When James Clarke, a Penrith surveyor, wrote *Survey of the Lakes* (1787) a boundary-stone was on some occasions still sacred, yet the number of hedges had mightly increased. "I know not that there can be a more remarkable passage in the history of rural civilisation, than the substitution of hedges in the place of the rude metes and boundaries so generally used in former times." Watchers of cattle became redundant. The effects of enclosing land were both scenic and commercial. Garnett, in *Westmorland Agriculture 1800-1900*, observed that commons had been capable only of half-starving the animals pastured upon them. Paring and burning, fencing and draining, liming, ploughing and sowing, had transformed the landscape – and increased the annual rental from between *6d* and *1s* per acre to one of from *20s* to *30s* per acre.

On the fells, stone was the handiest material for building and maintenance of boundaries. Walls were built to a standard height of 4 ft 6 inches with mutual help. Then skilled wallers were employed at up to thruppence an hour. So remote from habitations were some of the walls, the builders must have camped near their work for days on end. Large pieces of stone or slate were transported by horse-drawn sled, the stones being broken into convenient sizes on site. The walls were constructed without a dab of mortar. In 1845, a rood of wall cost eight shillings. Included in the price was the cost of gathering stone and carting it to the line of the wall. Wallers in Borrowdale received no more than 2s per day of 12 to 14 hours.

A Lakeland wall was, in fact, two walls in one, resting on large *footing stones* and held together by big stones known as *throughs*. Small *hearting stones* were carefully packed into spaces left between the two sections of the wall and the whole was capped with *cam stones*, which sloped at an angle of 45 degrees. At the head of a dale, the ground and the becks were littered with small rounded stones that had been trundled down from the fells through natural forces. At Wasdale Head, when the common field of 345 acres was split by walls, the worn stones were used with consummate skill and the surplus stones left in neat heaps, some of which were walled round. Where mixed grazing was intended, a *hogg-hole* was left at the base of a wall, permitting the passage of sheep but not cattle. A flagstone blocked the hole if the sheep were to be restricted.

Drystone walls lay in the dales like a futuristic pattern and then took to higher ground, each course being kept horizontal, even on the steepest ground. In Kentmere and Borrowdale, massive boulders were walled round. Some unenclosed fell commons remained after the walling frenzy. Such a common was usually *stinted* to regulate the number of animals being grazed, ensuring that vegetation would not be eaten bare. On Bassenthwaite Common, every farmer who had a *stint* [share of the common] was entitled to a lot or allotment [a fenced-off portion]. He was allotted one *cattle-gate* [about 15 acres] for every hundred sheep or thirty cows.

The fell on which the Coates family of Grange Farm, Borrowdale, ran their sheep was unhandy for the farm, being large and enclosed, lying off the Langstrath Valley. Here the farmer and his farm lad spent hours gap-walling. They took with them some food, also a kettle, which was set on a fire mainly composed of dry heather. E M Ward (1929) wrote that the course of recent agricultural history at the Lakes has been marked by the gradual extension of walls. She likened them to "a stony spider's web" and commented sadly that more recent history is reflected in their slow decay.

The Updale Chapels

D uring the 12th and 13th centuries, with a greatly increasing population, chapels were built in the dale-country as part of land clearance and settlement. The project was usually carried out by the lord of the manor or by someone to whom land had been granted. Patrick, son of Thomas de Workington, who built Thornthwaite chapel about the year 1240, used land granted to Thomas by Alice de Rumeli. The 16th century saw the building of chapels in remote places to spare the dalesfolk long, sometimes arduous journeys to a mother church.

Borrowdale had its chapel in 1505 and Ennerdale its place of worship in 1542. In the next decade, chapels were built at Wasdale Head and Wythburn. In pre-chapel days, the dead of Wasdale Head had been conveyed, on horse-drawn sled or strapped to a horse, over Burnmoor to St Catherine's, Eskdale. (In recent times, the tiny chapel at Wasdale Head was dedicated to St Olaf, Norway's patron saint). A map of 1576 showed chapels at Newlands, Mallerstang and Mungrisedale. References to Langdale and Long Sleddale appeared in 1571. When Sir George Rose dined with Lord Langdale, his host spoke of the tiny church in Langdale – a church of which he was patron – remarking that "it is not bigger than this dining room." Sir George added "...and the living is not half so good." Witherslack chapel was mentioned in an archbishop's visitation in 1578.

Matterdale was given parochial rights in 1580, the inhabitants having claimed that "from the annoyances of snow and other foul weather in the winter season in that fellish part they be often very sore troubled with carrying the dead corpses... and the infants there born unto burial or christening". The parish church was at Greystoke. Lakeland also had *corpse ways*, described by Rollinson as "jealously-guarded routes from farms to the church along which corpses were carried for burial, any deviation being regarded as an ill-omen. In Troutbeck (Westmorland) are records of fences being removed to allow a funeral procession to pass along a traditional route."

Until 1729, the dead of Mardale were strapped to the backs of horses and taken up the Corpse Road by Mardale Common and Swindale for burial at Shap. The first body to be buried at Mardale was that of John Turner of Mardale Green, who died in 1729. The last body to be borne over the fells was that of John Holme, of Brackenhowe, on 7 June, 1736. The parish clerk was not over-worked. Apart from Sundays, few services were held. A sexton grimly remarked: "Six full days and I'd bury everyone in the parish."

The updale parsons were characters who had to eke their miserably small stipends with a variety of other jobs. Among them was the Rev Mr Mattinson, curate at Patterdale from 1715 until 1763. Until the last years of his life – and this astonishing man lived to celebrate his 96th birthday – his stipend did not exceed £12 and never attained £20 per annum. He so improved his income by his industry and domestic economy that he saved £1,000. Mrs Mattinson charged a shilling for each birth she attended, also for "culinary perquisites", such as the cost of food eaten at christening parties. Prompt payment led to her wishing a mother a speedy recovery and an "early return of such blessings." Mattinson served at Patterdale long enough to bury his mother, marry and bury his father, christen his wife and publish his own banns of marriage. He christened and officiated at the weddings of all his four children.

Incidentally, a dish consumed at Lakeland christenings was *butter sops*. Joseph Budworth (1792) described how it was made. Wheat bread was cut into thin slices and placed in rows one above the other in a large kettle of 20 or 30 gallons. Butter and sugar were dissolved in a separate kettle and then poured upon the bread, "where it continues until it has boiled for some space and the bread is perfectly saturated with the mixture. It is then taken out and served up by way of a desert."

In about 1789, the curate of Langdale, in support of himself and his family, kept a tavern and sold ale. Parishioners augmented the curate's salary with voluntary contributions. The curate had an allowance of clothes, paid annually, these consisting of a new suit, two pairs of shoes, a pair of clogs and some stockings. A poor minister was allowed a *whittle-gate* – the privilege of going from house to house in his parish. He would stay for a certain number of days with each family and entered his *whittle* [knife] into the common dish. At that time, knives were not common; few houses had more than one or two. In the humblest abode, the curate might also share a bed with one or other of the family.

Robert Walker, the parson at Seathwaite, in the Duddon Valley, was a prime example of how, when his living did not quite measure up to the name, he set about augmenting his income. The Seathwaite chapel register, recording his death in 1802, observed "he was a man singular for his temperance, industry and integrity." Walker was born in 1709 and, being a delicate child, became the scholar of his family, finding employment as schoolmaster at Loweswater and elsewhere in Cumberland. He received the cost of travelling, also bed and board, as part of his wages from the parents of his scholars. Qualifying for Holy Orders, in 1735, he accepted the curacy of Seathwaite at a salary of £5 per annum, in which the use of a cottage was included. Partnered by a like-minded wife, he reared a large family on the proceeds of his parsimony rather than on the income from his curacy, though this he increased from £5 to £17 a year. When he died, he was worth £2,000.

An account of his life is an insight into life in the Lakeland dales in the 18th century. Walker's school was in the church. He taught from the Communion table and simultaneously was busy at his spinning wheel. He had a small farm and assisted his neighbours. He was lawyer, accountant, doctor and general factotum to his widely scattered parishioners. At one time farming at Gateskill, at the far end of the Duddon Valley, on his death in June, 1802, aged 92, a curious block of stone on which he sat when clipping sheep was transferred to his burial place at Seathwaite churchyard.

In 1820, William Wordsworth wrote a pen portrait of Walker, describing him as frugal, temperate and energetic to the extent of finding time after preaching and teaching to assist his neighbours to make hay and clip sheep. "Once a month, during the proper season, a sheep was drawn from their small mountain flock and killed for the use of the family; and a cow, towards the close of the year, was salted and dried for winter provision: the hide was tanned to furnish them with shoes." When tea came into general use, it was offered to visitors and members of the family who lived elsewhere but paid a return visit to the family home. Neither the curate nor his wife had ever drunk tea, which religious folk at the time were inclined to think of an a drug from the Orient.

Up to the 19th century, the little churches of the Lake District were frequently used as schools. Cock-fighting was popular and money was waged upon it. An example of a cock-pits existing near a church is to be found at St John's in the Vale, near Thirlmere. Men who had not been ordained were permitted to hold Lakeland cures until Georgian times. They became deacons and were addressed as "Sir". At the beginning of the eighteenth century, Bishop Nicholson observed "there was not a curate in any chapel who was not called 'Sir'." According to Robert Southey, the curate of Newlands, near Keswick, augmented his income through work as tailor, clogger and butter-print maker. A word picture of the village curate appears in *Dutch Agnes*, a novel by W G Collingwood. The story concerns denizens at Hawkshead and Coniston. The main occupation of Collingwood's curate was that of village schoolmaster who scrubbed the floors and cleaned the windows of church and schoolhouse.

A curate needed the income from some other occupation. A chapelry's worth might not exceed two or three pounds a year. Richard Birkett, who served the chapel of Martindale for 67 years, had an endowment of £2.14s.4d a year, plus a small house and four acres of land. The Easter dues were paid in eggs. At this time, Birkett carried a board with a hole cut into it. It formed a gauge and he rejected any eggs that passed through it.

Parson Sewell, of Troutbeck, the schoolmaster at Ambleside, also kept the inn at the summit of the Kirkstone Pass. During a drought, when the Bishop urged the clergy to pray for rain, Sewell remarked: "What's use o' praying for rain wi' t'wind comen out o' Blue Gill?" He was preaching at Wythburn, using a rickety pulpit, when his sermon slipped in a crack that had appeared between pulpit and wall. He could not retrieve his notes and announced that "I'll read ye a chapter o' t'Bible worth ten of it." A Mr Sherwen, who died in 1870, was noted for his long sermons, during the course of one of which he said: "And what shall I say next?" A member of the congregation called out "Amen!"

Sheep-clipping stool used by Robert Walker

The Indomitable Herdwick

As related, the little herdwick sheep was *heaf*-going. It rarely strayed from the patch of ground on which it had grown up. Authorities are divided about the derivation of the word *heaf*. Canon H D Rawnsley, vicar of Crosthwaite, near Keswick, quoted the Icelandic *hefd* or *hefda*, meaning a place of possession by prescriptive right. A Great Langdale farmer simplified the concept by saying: "Some of the sheep I sold came back to have another look at us." One sheep returned from Waterside, Ullswater, to Eskdale. Nine sheep sold from Eskdale and taken to Ullswater in the early spring, returned to their natal area in Eskdale – with their lambs.

If the herdwicks were *heafed*, so were the families who owned them. William Wilson, better-known as Herdwick Billy because of his knowledge of the breed, was born at Wood How Farm, Nether Wasdale, a farm that was leased along with 400 herdwick sheep. He then spent twenty years of his farm life at Watendlath, tending 3,000 sheep of the native breed. He had such a regard for herdwicks at his last Lakeland home, near the outflow of Bassenthwaite Lake, the image of a herdwick was fixed in stained glass for a window in the porch. As noted, he had known a custom called *clouting the twinters*. Shearlings that were too young to be put to the tup had *clouts* [small pieces of cloth, made from old clothes or coarse sacking] placed at their rumps. It was a form of birth control. The cloths, removed in spring, were washed and ironed so as to be ready for another mating season.

An individualistic streak is found in the herdwick. Nancy Price (1935) heard shepherds calling some of the tups by names relating to peculiar characteristics – names such as White Top, Blue Top, Crag and Hard Nut, the last being "a difficult fellow to manage." Sheep with ancestors in the Bronze Age were improved by selective breeding, being tidied up in the late 18th and early 19th centuries. H H Symonds, commenting on herdwicks, mentioned "the sneeze, half friendly, half contemptuous, with which they greet the passer-by in lonely places."

S D Stanley-Dodgson, writing in the First (1920) Flock Book of the breeders' association, described a typical herdwick sheep as one that primarily had a good strong cost of flowing wool, well carried out over the chest and hind legs and the underside or belly well covered. The head should be carried high, "broad across the forehead, deep in the jaw, wide at the nostrils, arched nose, and with a bold, prominent, well developed eye. The ears should be white and sharp, well set up and active, like those of a well-bred horse."

The face of a typical herdwick should be "grey or rimy (hoar-frosted in appearance)". The ideal body was "round and deep; chest prominent and wide; legs covered with strong bristly hair, set well outside; knees strong, short from knee to fetlock; a good spring fetlock; and wide white foot; tail thick at the root, reaching to the hocks and well-covered with strong wool." Dark-coloured sheep were preferred, "as showing constitutions and fitness for mountain life." Breeders might often be heard to say that they rarely found a *breuked* [dark grey] sheep a bad doer. Spotted legs and faces were inadmissible.

Samuel Barber (1892) wrote there was no question as to the quality of their mutton, which was well flavoured and nutritious. The flesh was without extra fat, "which is doubtless removed by lively exercise upon the fells." The Rev H H Symonds (1937) believed that "in wits and strength the herdwick outdoes all other breeds of sheep and is the irreplaceable source of local wealth and welfare." To Allan Fraser, author of *Sheep Husbandry* (1949) the herdwick is a true hill breed, white-faced, horns on tup only, with rough fleece of carpet-wool class, the body deep and round. "It is reputed, like members of a certain Highland clan, to possess an extra rib."

Mary Fair, of Holmrook, who was captivated by the herd-wick breed, believed that the breed originated in a stock that found its way into the area in prehistoric times and roamed more or less wild until it was domesticated in Celtic times. She noted that the garrisons of the Roman forts on Hadrian's Wall had a partiality for mutton, much of which would be provided from native sources. Bill Rollinson, historian, assessed that the most common breed of sheep was probably a cross between a small, black-faced, indigenous variety and the herdwick. Each ewe seldom produced more than one lamb. The coarse fleece weighed about three to four pounds. A Lakeland farmer attested that the wool should neither be soft nor too hard; there should be "a decent jacket wi' a bit o' waistcoat in it to keep the storm out."

Many a Lakeland family lived off their sheep. Farmers slaughtered old *wethers* [castrated sheep] and dried the flesh, just like the ham of a pig, when it became known as *makin*. "Salted leg", which dangled from many a kitchen beam, was so called because "you put a lile bit o' saltpetre on the bone end and salt on the flesh." At Christmas, *sweet pie* was made from bits of fatty mutton, being presented in a large dish with a thin crust. Sheep's head broth was a cheap delicacy at a time when the head was obtainable from the local butcher for sixpence. Sheepskin, cured with saltpetre and alum, served as rugs or mats. Some skins were worn as *brats* [aprons] at dipping time. The fat from slaughtered herdwicks was rendered down and used for candle making or to weatherproof boots.

A typical herdwick farm has a limited amount of dale and extensive fell grazings. The flock was composed of ewes, ewe shearlings, *hoggs* [last year's lambs] *wethers* [castrated animals] and rams. An old-time farmer expected a mature herdwick to fend for itself. Only the *hoggs* were provided with additional food, being fed hay in simple structures known as *hogghouses*. B L Thompson, of the National Trust, for long the major owner of herdwick sheep, believed that leaves of holly and branches of thorn were collected to be browsed by the *hoggs*. Norse terms used by Lakeland farmers include *gimmer* [a female sheep] and *twinter* [a two-year-old]. *Lug* [ear] might be a corruption of the word law, for a sheep's lugs were clipped in a distinctive way as a mark of ownership. Smit marks featured the owner's initials and a distinctive mark, as noted in *The Shepherd's Guide*, which was first published in the 19th century. A farm called Raven Crag had a mark featuring a drawing of a bird's foot.

Exposed to damp winds from the west, and periodically drenched by heavy rain, the herdwick's fleece might be of low value but was capable of drying out more quickly than that of a white-woolled breed. The herdwick ram, wrote Mary Fair, is a long-tailed sheep; his frosty grey-white face is as typical as it is attractive; his harsh grey overcoat, with the soft creamy-white undercoat, make splendid weather-resisting tweeds and stockings. Sheep have the good sense to migrate to lower ground in anticipation of a heavy snowfall. Sheep find good shelter in the lee of drystone walls. In 1939-40 the walls in upper Borrowdale were overblown. Some 30 or 40 sheep perished at Seathwaite Farm. In 1947, the snowfall here was not as great and the dale road was never closed but conditions on the fells were grim. The death toll of sheep was about 400.

Joseph Gregg, who farmed in Great Langdale, graded herd-wick ewes in 1952, following a good spring and summer, and thirty of them averaged 1 cwt. Some had suckled two lambs on the fells. A couple of gimmer lambs won at Smithfield in 1973. Their live weights averaged 170 lb. Joseph had known a hogg weigh 184 lb, though it was brought up as a pet, being run only on the best land "and pinching what it could from the farmyard!" Having clipped 8 lb of wool off a sheep, he sent the wool to a firm in the north that specialised in making up suits. The herdwick suit was as good as a raincoat. "One day I walked from Eskdale to get the morning bus to Elterwater.

When I'd left the bus, I'd to walk over Wrynose and Hardknott passes. It was raining all the time but at the end of the walk I took off that Herdwick suit and just shook it. The cloth was as dry as when I'd set off."

The fells do not carry as many herdwick sheep as formerly. Fifty years ago, the Richardsons of Gatesgarth, between Buttermere and Honister, had 130 acres of *inland* and around 2,500 acres of fell, from Scale Force to the edge of Green Gable, whereon might be found four stocks of herdwicks. The stocking rate was "roughly one sheep per acre." Each stock had a name, examples being Scale Force, Burtness, Fleetwith and Gatesgarth Side (known to the farmer simply as Honister). John Fletcher Buntin, who kept herdwicks in Great Langdale, recalled the loss of eight stocks of sheep belonging to different Grasmere farmers from this area alone. "There must be over 700 fewer sheep on Bowfell."

The old-time Lakeland calendar began in October when fresh tups were needed for a "change of blood." They were hired, not bought at Keswick or Eshd'l [Eskdale] showground, the Eskdale event being known as the Herdwick Royal. Farmers adorned their best sheep with "red rudd" and in later days with reddish powder that came in a packet and was let down with light oil. Applied to a fleece, it gave the sheep a rusty tinge. This did not serve any practical purpose; it was simply traditional to "improve t'look of 'em." The wool merchants preferred the fleeces to be in "natural colour."

A farmer looked for a sheep that appeared clean, with a bit o' bone, good colour and plenty of wool. A conversation between two farmers might run something like this: "Whoo's ta gooing on today? Hesta any tips to part wid?" "Well, ev yan or two." "This 'esn't mich coat on it." "It's reight enuff." "Whoo mich ista wanting for it?" "Thirty bob." "I'll gie thee twenty-five bob." "Split it." "Reight." A handclasp sealed the bargain.

At the Eskdale Show of 1961, farmers hired some 300 tups

Continued on page 57

Above and left: Farmers attending the Herdwick Royal (Eskdale).
Right: a farmer in remote little Martindale.

Above: Sheepdogs await their turn at Wasdale Head trials.
Below: Peggy Ellwood, in her kitchen in the Duddon Valley.

Above: Fell ponies share hay with Swaledale sheep, Askham Common.
Below: Isolated cottages "back o' Skiddaw."

Two old-time studies of Seathwaite, reputedly the "wettest spot in England," which occupies its own little valley extending from the head of Borrowdale.

Little churches. Above: St Kentigern's, in Mungrisedale.
Below: Interior of Wythburn church, a building standing at the foot of Helvellyn.

"Humble if is, and meek, and very low,
And speaks its purpose by a single bell:
But God Himself, and He alone, can know
If spiry temples please Him half so well."
Coleridge.

Drystone walling at Wasdale Head, where the stones tend to be rounded and not easy to use. In the background is Great Gable, from near the summit of which the web-like pattern of Wasdale walls may be admired.

for the winter. Sometimes tups were sold privately. Then you might see the spectacle of *hand-slapping* to seal a bargain. Nothing has been written down. No Lakeland farmer would think of going back on his word. Traditionally, on the Sunday before Eskdale Show-day, some farmers went on the rounds of farms where suitable tups were bred. It was known as Tup Sunday. The show was held in such respect that sheep were walked here from all parts of the Lake District, their proud owners spending three or four days away from home. Wasdale sheep came over Burnmoor. Those from Langdale used Wrynose and Hardknott passes. Broughton stock was driven across Birker Moor. Joe Teasdale, of Caldbeck, brought a tup to Eskdale in a horse-drawn cart.

Farmers kept the hired tups until the first Friday in May, returning them to a spring show in the same field. Sometimes tups were sold privately. Fifty years ago, the hire charge varied between 25s and 30s and it cost up to £40 to purchase a tup outright. Forty years ago, a good tup might be valued at £50, even £100, but the hiring fee would be somewhere between £2 and £4. "A lot goes on friendship," said a Langdale farmer. "If you *ken* [know] the owner, or even his neighbour, he might hire out a tup for nowt."

In late November, the tups had their way with ewes that had been brought from the fell to the *in-bye* [valley bottom] land. The ewes would return to the fell about a month after tupping. A shepherd was "amang 'em" once a fortnight, taking in those that were not thriving. In April and May, ewes lambed on the in-bye. A herdwick tends to need a lot of attention at lambing time. "A ewe's so proud it keeps backin' away. The lamb never gets a chance." A shepherd going his round on a cold, wet morning knew the conditions as "a real tickler". It was vital for a lamb to take milk from the ewe as soon as possible. In difficulty, a ewe was firmly held and the lamb placed in position to suck. The tail root was tickled to stimulate the lamb to drink.

Ewes with single lambs are taken back to the fell in May. The sheep with twin lambs remain on the low ground until after the June clipping. Spaining [the separation of ewes from lambs after weaning] occurs place in September. The ewes retained for breeding are sent back to the fell and spare sheep are *drafted* – sold to lowland farmers for crossing with mutton-producing strains. In October, most of the wether lambs are sold *store* to lowland farmers to fatten. In November, gimmer [ewe] lambs go to lowland farms on their winter "holiday".

This custom began towards the end of the 19th century, when hoggs were being wintered on the coastal flats beside the Solway and Morecambe Bay. John Hind, employed at Grange Farm, Borrowdale just before the First World War, remembered when some 600 hoggs were taken to Solway shore from the huge Seathwaite Farm at the head of the valley. The operation of moving them might take a fortnight. Farmers and their men stayed the night at different farms their families had patronised for many years. A century ago, the cost of wintering was five shillings a head. By mid-20th century, the maintenance cost had risen to twenty-five shillings. With a greater emphasis on their dairy herds, farmers preferred to keep the pasture clear of stock to provide an early bite for the cattle.

When a herdwick ewe has produced lambs over three or four years, it is drafted from the fell to low ground and here, being active, strong-boned and of a good conformation, the draft ewe is crossed with mutton-producing strains to yield sound cross-bred lambs. Upper dales farms, especially those bequeathed by Beatrix Potter to the National Park, retained stocks of herdwick sheep. Elsewhere, the Swaledale breed has become evident. The demand was for sheep of larger size, with softer wool, larger joints of meat and maturing quicker for market were becoming available. Old-time farmers shook their heads and forecast that in a grim winter only the herdwick stock would thrive.

Salving. An old saying has been mis-quoted. You saved a sheep, not a ship, with a ha'porth of tar. As soon as the back-end came, flockmasters began to think of *salving* their flocks against the dreaded scourge of scab and to proof the fell-going sheep against winter storms. Salving was done by systematically parting the wool the length of the sheep, one *shed* after another. Salve kept in a wooden bowl attached to the stool on which the salver sat was applied via the operative's first finger. Every inch of the sheep was covered.

In 1646, Sir Daniel Fleming of Rydal paid £3.11s.2d to have his flock salved, using a mixture of butter, tallow and tar. The cost of the salve was considerable: 31 stones of butter, £6.10s; 8 stones of tallow, £2.23.4d; and 3½ loads of tar, £4.10s. An advertisement of 1869 reads: "To agriculturalists., etc., Christopher Mayson, Seedsman, Tallow Chandler, Dealer in Butter and Tar, Market Place, Cockermouth. Always on hand for the season. Butter and Tar Shinner's grease." The grease made the salve set after it had been mixed hot. In later days, salve was made of Stockholm tar and Skinner grease. Very little tar was needed. Sometimes, the grease used would be home-made butter – stuff that could not be sold or which had deteriorated. There were professional salvers. A doctor, who counted the sheds by parting the wool downwards, checked their work.

Most big farms had a salving house where work went on well into the night. Of the four to five pounds of fat in a slaughtered sheep, some was used to make candles that were clipped to the nebs of caps worn by farm men as they handled the sheep after dark during salving time. A week would be devoted to making candles. The old way was to get a piece of metal, somewhat bigger than a knitting needle, and tie to it pieces of *tow* [wick]. They were allowed to settle in a pot of fat that was kept hot. When they were withdrawn, fat clung to the pieces of tow and when dried, they were dipped again. Gradually, a sufficient thickness of fat was built up. If candles were kept for a long time, they began to flake. A good salver dealt with from seven to 12 animals a day, so an average hill flock could not be salved in under three weeks.

When Joseph Gregg was a nipper at the turn of the 19th century, he watched men who were salving herdwick sheep. "Every farm had a salving house. Salving went on after dark, by lamplight. We didn't talk about eight-hour days then, you know.

The last traces of salve departed when the sheep were washed before clipping. A beck was dammed. The washer, who was wading up to his waist, had sheep thrown to him from the bank. A faint trace of salve entered the water and stupefied the trout. Salving ended early in the 20th century when *sheep-dipping* became compulsory.

Herdwick

Rough Fell Sheep

This breed, found mainly on the slaty eastern fells, such as the Howgills, underpinned Kendal's wool trade at a time when the grey town's motto was "wool is my bread". The only guide we have to the breed's origins is an observation of George Culley in 1794. A Rough Fell had spiral horns, black faces and black legs, and fierce and wild-looking eyes. It had "a short, firm carcass... covered with long, open, coarse wool; the fleeces weighed from 3½ to 4 lbs each and sold in 1792 for 6d per lb."

Lowe (1842), supporting a notion that Rough Fell breed had its origin in Cumberland and Westmorland, noted that travelling north it had become the foundation of the Scotch Blackfaced breed. Also termed the Blackfaced Heath breed, "it extends across the vales of Kendal and Eden to the higher mountains of Cumberland and Westmorland in the west and by the Carter Fell into Scotland... During the past century the Blackfaced Heath or Muir sheep has been gradually improved, its development proceeding along different lines, resulting in three distinct varieties being evolved in the county, viz: Scotch, Rough Fell and Swaledale."

Garnett, in his *Westmorland Agriculture, 1800-1900* (1912), supposed that the sheep of the county were descended from the Black-faced Heath sheep. By crossing with some other kinds – with Herdwicks in the West, Cheviots in the North and the Crag sheep of the South, different types were evolved. Even today, these were peculiar to their particular districts. "Some of them have a large portion of white in their face and legs; some have these parts speckled and others, totally black; they are, in general, horned, high-shouldered, narrow backed, flat side, strong boned, and many with thick rough, hairy legs. The wool is coarse and long."

Rough Fell sheep were noted for carrying a large amount of wool, some 5 lb on average. Fleeces that weighed double that weight were not rare. In the impoverished years of the early 1930s, wool sold at 4d a lb, representing a wool cheque of about £150 a farm. A breeders' association, formed in 1927, led to improvements. The type changed from being blackfaced, with grey nose and an especially strong fleece, to black and white "bald" face and much softer wool. The breed has stamina, as testified by Bob Thompson, who farmed Stockdale, in the Rough Fell Country. He saw a fox sitting on the snow, staring fixedly at a snowbound sheep. Rescuing the weakened sheep, the farmer put it in the barn and gave it new milk, morning and night, for three weeks. "It went on champion."

Rough Fell

Shepherds and Sheepdogs

Jonathan Otley wrote: "In the summer season... the flocks ascend their steeps and nibble a scanty sustenance from the blades of grass peeping out between the stones on the highest summits. Some of the sheep are annually drawn from the flock and placed in the enclosures to fatten – and they make excellent mutton; but many remain upon commons during winter when, in deep snows, the occupation of the shepherd becomes arduous." Canon Rawnsley (1903) told of an old man who had "struggled with storm on Skiddaw through his laborious life, failed in health, suffered as shepherds often do from terrible rheumatism and was troubled with asthma. At last he felt obliged to leave the ingle-nook and take to his bed upstairs. His love of the shepherd's life was still so strong upon him that a few days before he died he insisted on seeing one of his prized herdwick rams." The sons had a tough job getting it into the presence of the dying man who, on seeing the tup, said he was "ready to gang home."

Rawnsley's "old man" was Edward Hawell, one of those commemorated on a stone cross that stands on the low ridge of Latrigg and is seen by those who ascend Skiddaw. The Hawells, who lived at Lonsdale Farm, were noted breeders of prize herdwick sheep. Originally there were two names upon it, these being of Edward Hawell, of Lonsdale, born October 21st, 1815, died June 2nd, 1889, and his son Joseph Hawell, of Lonsdale, born December 24, 1854, died February 20th, 1891. The shaft is adorned with "the endless knot their Norse forefathers used, in symbol of eternity," to quote Rawnsley, who composed the verse that is let into the base of the memorial:

Great Shepherd of Thy Heavenly Flock

These men have left our hill,
Their feet were on the living rock
Oh, guide and bless them still.

Also inscribed on the base is the name of Robert Walker Hawell, born 16th March, 1851, died 29th December, 191l. At their zenith, the Hawells had a Herdwick prize room, the walls of which were covered by prizes and cards. James Telford, a jeweller at Keswick, as a young man, visited Lonsdale to attend to the clocks. He walked to the farm with his tools and reported to his family and friends that in the hall of the farm stood four stuffed rams. The celebrated *Shepherd's Guide*, revised by R H Lamb in 1937, includes the marks of over 1,000 Lakeland flocks. Mrs Williamson's flock at Routen might be distinguished by a "cropped near ear, under fold bited far ear, pop on far hook". A sheep in George Kirkby's flock at Beckside was "cropped and under key-bitted near, under halfed far, three shot strokes over back".

Shepherds became accustomed to their own company. Leslie Grisedale, who for six years worked on Shap Fell, over 1,000 ft above sea level, had the care of 500 sheep on an equivalent number of acres. His home was half a mile from the next habitation. The Lakeland shepherd was an adroit cragsman. Herbert Grisedale, of Langdale, told that in early spring, when the sweetest grass grew in out-of-the-way places, a few sheep that ventured on to the ledges of crags were unable to find a way back. They were said to be cragfast. To a sheep's rescue went three men with a hemp rope about 60 ft long. They also carried a finer "draw" rope – and had a pocketful of small stones.

When one man, lowered down the crag face, was dangling about eight feet above the ledge on which the sheep was trapped, he pitched stones on either side to remind the sheep of its precarious position. The draw rope had a noose at one end. The ropeman had a stick into which a nail was driven. From it the small rope was allowed to dangle as he tried to get the noose over the sheep's head. When the sheep was secured, its legs were bound and it was ready to be drawn up the crag to safety.

Lakeland sheep farming would be difficult without the aid of a collie, the name for the most the most popular breed. It is a Celtic term meaning "useful". A shepherd needed one or more dogs. Until the 1820s, there was an almost bewildering variety – hounds, pointers, spaniels, lurchers and greyhounds. When there was an outbreak of rabies in 1824, the Mayor of Kendal ordered that all dogs were to be fastened up. Six years later, the Mayor issued a notice that "no person need for apprehensive of the consequences of destroying dogs running about the streets." In 1841, at Appleby, the Mayor instructed the bellman to announce that all dogs found at large would be destroyed.

What the Lakeland shepherd needed was a dog with strength and intelligence that had the ability to control sheep. Old Hemp (1893-1901), who matched that requirement, is regarded as the ancestor of the Border Collie breed, which was found on either side of the national border. A hill collie must have a good wide run on the fell, giving the sheep plenty of room. A dog that is always on the move might cover fifty miles of fell in a day. Joe Relph, who lived near Keswick, used to say: "Some people consider that sheep are not intelligent. My experience is that they are very clever. Sheep will quickly notice any weakness in the dog." Some dogs were *high dogs* – the stars in sheepdog trials. Such a dog was "aw reet in t'fields but lost when it has to work on t'fells, among rough stones and bracken."

Isaac Myers, of Wall End, Great Langdale, bred his own sheepdogs. He had three – Meg, Fly and Bright. His shepherd worked Nell and Ted. Short names for dogs were chosen so as to be shoutable. "Best dog I had was two afore it started work," said Isaac. "I thought it was going to be a dud, but when it got going it didn't need training. And it worked till it was eleven years old." The best dogs are said to work for one master. Isaac had such a dog. "If I let a pup out with it, it wouldn't work. It'd just sulk. You see, it's a stylish worker. A puppy maks a mess o' things."

With thousands of sheep on wall-less fells, it was inevitable that when a farmer gathered his stock he would also take up one or two strays. The stock of sheep belonging to Gatesgarth, at the head of Buttermere, edged up to stocks from Wasdale, Ennerdale, Borrowdale, Newlands and Loweswater. Strays were restored to their owners at Shepherds' Meets. A Meet held at Bampton, on the eastern side of the fells, had taken the place of the historic meet held at the *Dun Bull*, Mardale, until it went under the chilling waters of a Manchester reservoir. Isaac Hinchliffe, in *A Backwater in Lakeland*, a book about Mardale published in 1925, mentioned that for nearly a century there had been an annual Shepherds' Meet at the *Dun Bull* during the third week in November. "In the old days this meet was held on the top of High Street, accompanied by horse-racing and the usual sports of those days. Imagine toiling from Mardale, Kentmere, Patterdale and even far-away Longsleddale, rising 2,000 ft or so over rough ground, carrying barrels of beer and other things necessary for a feast."

Shepherds' Meets were held in the autumn at Wasdale Head, Buttermere, Thirlspot and Matterdale (in alternative years), Mungrisedale (among the Skiddaw fells) and outside the *Travellers' Rest*, by Kirkstone Pass, 1,500 ft above sea level. The last-named venue was moved to the *Queen's Arms* at Troutbeck. Custom once decreed that a man who did not turn up to claim a sheep was fined a small sum. Forty years ago, the strays included Rough Fell, Swaledale and Dales-bred sheep. Farmers who were down on their count of sheep moved among the sheep looking for their markings that would be undeniable evidence of ownership. One of the largest batches usually came from the nearby Troutbeck Park, one of Beatrix Potter's farms, which was said to have "2,000 acres of sheep".

Inside the inn, with the business of the day over, farmers and shepherds talked, drank, then sang until their throats were dry – and drank again. When a hot-pot was cooked, everyone tramped up the stairs to the Mayor's Parlour, The sight that greeted them was a long table set out with cutlery and huge jars of pickles, piccalilli and beetroot. The hot-pot, thick and sustaining, was a Westmorland blend of meat and other savoury foodstuffs. There followed a helping of pie and custard, the whole washed down by strong tea. In the evening, the inn rang with laughter, tale-telling and song.

The shepherd had to be alert to ailing sheep. Sheep complaints had quaint names. Rawnsley wrote about the *blow-fly*, also known as *mawk* or *wick*, which used a sheep as a repository for its eggs and was most active in thundery weather, when then was insufficient sunshine to dry the fleece quickly. A smitten sheep tended to skulk in bracken or among rocks and could be closely approached. Nothing could be more pitiable to Canon Rawnsley than "the distressful condition of a sheep bearing about in its body the living plague of the thousands of eggs deposited within its wounded being." A *souted* sheep was one that had indulged too freely on the common upland plant known as cotton grass, which is actually a sedge. The sheep usually recovered when it was given a change of pasture. Rawnsley was fascinated by *sturdy*, a name said to be derived from the French etourdi, meaning giddy. The complaint was caused when a bladder of grubs formed on one side of the brain of a sheep, putting its neck on one side and causing the animal to constantly spin on its axis. A skilled shepherd, using a red-hot iron, drove a hole in the skull and deftly removed the small bladder containing the parasites. By late Victorian times, sturdy was being tackled by making an incision with a sharp knife to lay the brain bare in the affected part. The bladder was extracted after a feather had been bent round it and the wound bound by cloth or tar plaster.

Gatesgarth

The Boon Clip

To our clippings we'll invite each good merry soul,
And the master be joyful and say,
Be hearty and cheerful o'er a good flowing bowl,
And we'll drink till the dawn of the day.

Thus begins a clipping song that was popular in Martindale, a valley tucked away among lonely fells near Ullswater. In the seventeenth century, when yeoman farmers were proudly self-sufficient, fleeces from the sheep might be spun into yarn which, collected by the *chapman* [carrier] were conveyed to a local weaver. Kendal's importance was based largely on the woollen trade, the wool being clipped from the sheep in the season from mid-June to mid-July. The fleeces, neatly folded, were stored under cover for sale in the autumn. The fleece from a herdwick ewe yielded about 3 lb and a *wether* up to six or seven pounds. A tup fleece was considerably heavier.

A fortnight before clipping day, the local beck was dammed, using stones, soil, even old doors. Sheep were tossed into the dub, grabbed by a man standing waist deep in water and had their fleeces ruffled to relieve them of dirt picked up on the fells. The washing process releasing traces of salve. Trout were stupefied and easily caught but were not fit to eat, having a tarry taste. A sheep must be dry when shorn. Rain-soaked wool becomes *foisty*, having a strong and unpleasant smell.

A *boon clip* was when each farm in turn had an appointed day and clipping became a co-operative effort. First, there was the gathering. Some of the big nineteenth century fell farms had over a thousand sheep. Collie dogs, giving mouth, roused laggard sheep from beds of bracken or alerted a farmer where a sheep was *rigged* [lying on its back]. A writer of 1870 remembered the *boon clip* as a time when, with farmers coming together, there was usually a good deal of arguing about which had the best tup, "but it is all agreeably settled over a glass and the pipe." They laboured, hard and long, clipping sheep and "pass the rest of the time with cheerful bits of songs and in drinking 'Confusion to the Scab' and 'Pack sheets and ready money' until the barrel of nut-brown ale is ready for turning at last." On some large farms, men devoted their time to catching sheep for the shearers; others collected shorn sheep to re-mark and dip them or to carry out minor operations such as sawing off the tip of a horn that was growing too close to a sheep's skull. The *creels* were made of larch by a local joiner.

Samuel Barber (1892) wrote: "To sit the whole of a hot summer day with sheep after sheep on one's knee, plying the shears, is certainly not the easiest business in the world, nor yet the lightest, and that a Merry Night should ensue upon it appears inevitable. A good supper, and afterwards a good talk on the day's proceedings, then a song or two by some benevolent amateur, and the evening begins. The instrument, violin or melodeon, is brought forth, the beer arrives and the ancient process of drinking the shepherd's health follows." A W Rumney, in his book *The Dalesman* (1911), related how Young Thompson and Edmondson, who had been to the Royal Show, had seen a sheep-shearing machine at work. They ridiculed a contraption for which a man provided the power by driving a stationary bicycle wheel and another guided the shears. The dalesmen were willing to back themselves against a machine with its two manipulators. If the sheep were to be herdwicks, they would give it a dozen start.

The clipping season at Gillerthwaite, in Ennerdale, involved between 2,000 and 3,000 sheep, which were tackled by over 20 shearers. They sat in a circle and were regaled with beer drawn from barrels. A small army of men provided them with sheep and took away those that had been shown. If a shearer was in need of a sheep, he would shout "Billy Ben", after an

old-time shepherd of that name. Though he had died generations before, he was still in everyone's minds. The mid-day
meal at Gillerthwaite was memorable. In the evening, wrestling
and various other sports took place, attracting young men
from a large part of West Cumberland.

At Middleton Hall, a huge farm by the upper Lune, clipping
took place about the 6th day of July. About sixty clippers
assembled, with yet more men catching, re-marking and
doctoring sheep feet. At night there would be a dance in the
empty barn. At Kentmere Hall before the First World War
preparations for the "boon clip" included the assembly in the
yard of about forty *creels* [stools cable of holding shearer and
sheep]. A hard day's work ended with a Clipping Party in an
outbuilding, with music provided by melodeon, played by
Noble Gregg.

The 1914-18 war had a profound effect on the way of life
in the Lakeland dales. Frank Birkett, of Braegarth, near Chapel
Stile, had vivid memories of the time when the "boon clip" was
an outstanding event attended by neighbours and friends. "It
was never the same after the war, when there were hardly any
men left. Those who remained did the best they could." Fell
Foot, Birk Howe and Base Brown were but three farms in the
Langdales noted for their "boon clip." "One man helped
another. A couple o' fellers clipping by hand some 800 sheep,
having had to gather them as well, would have to spread the
work over a month. It was different when there were many
willing hands."

Mr Birkett's father, who worked for Noble Bland at Middle
Fell Farm, was "tired out... gathering, clipping and dancing.
He didn't go to bed for three weeks." There was a knack in
wrapping fleeces. A "dab hand" was Old Ikie Morris, from
Pickles, the wool merchants of Kendal. Some Langdale farmers
transported their wool by horse and cart to Bennetts, the
carriers of Ambleside. *Shelvings*, a light frame, increased a
cart's capacity. Messrs Bennett, in turn, transported wool to

Kendal.

Mrs Birkett remembered when women made their rounds every two hours, providing the workers with beer from a jug, tea or sandwiches made of home-cured ham. A cold buffet was available at dinner-time. A hot meal was served in the evening. "When they had finished, at about six o'clock, the men went to some shallow tubs of warm water. Having stripped down to their waists, they had a good wash, then replaced their shirts, put on collars and ties and sat down to a big 'hot pot' before dancing most of the night away. At Troutbeck Park, Thomas Yewdale played his melodeon for dancing. The dance ended at about 4 a.m., when Thomas gently played *Now the Day is Over*."

The author, visiting Gatesgarth, between Buttermere and Honister, when the Richardsons had four stocks of herdwicks, totalling 2,500 sheep, heard that eight dogs helped with the gathering but only three men clipped, re-marked and dipped the animals. Within close range were medicines, in case a sheep was accidentally nicked or had some complaint, also a collection of marking fluids. A swim-bath contained an insect-stinging dose of Battle's Improved Summer Fly Dip or some other patent liquid that was effective against bites by *wicks*.

A herdwick being clipped must be kept under control for a struggling sheep might injure a man – or itself. The blades of the shears were sprung rather than pivoted, as with scissors and were "as deadly as rapiers". At smaller farms, the work would be done by about a dozen clippers. There might be forty men employed in this work at larger farms. Lambing ewes were the most difficult to clip. "You'd have a gay good do if you got an inch rise of new wool." The rise of new wool on the hoggs, wethers and geld sheep might be two inches and clipping them took less time. A novice at sheep shearing might "rive 'issen" in bits.

A sheep was first clipped around the breast, back legs and neck. Then the shears operated along one side up to the spine, at which stage the animal was turned so that the other side could receive attention. Wool from around the tail was clipped away. An expert could clip a sheep in around five minutes. A fleece was rolled up and neatly tied, using a band made from part of the wool that had been deftly twisted.

In marking sheep after clipping, generous use was made of red ruddle or tar, despite the laments of merchants and mill-owners that tar would not scour out. The sheep-clipping song, which William Greenhow, shepherd to Hugh Holme, last "king" of Mardale, sang to the tune of the *Old Hundredth*, without accompaniment, began:

> *Tarry woo', oh! tarry woo',*
> *Tarry woo' is ill to spin;*
> *Card it well, oh! card it well,*
> *Card it well ere ye begin.*

Tarry woo' was the wool left by the sheep on rough vegetation, trees and walls – wool that the thrifty shepherds collected. The use of tar as a marker was eventually phased out. Old Isaac Myers, of Great Langdale, found the Bradford dyes satisfactory but when he applied some Australian dye it stayed on the fleece for only a fortnight. An old marking mixture was tar and a paste made from a deeply-coloured ore gathered at Red Tarn.

Half a century ago, Sydney Moorhouse described when the gates of the clipping yard were opened and ewes were re-united with their lambs. "For a time chaos reigns. Lambs dash here and there. Ewes sniff first one, then another, rejecting many until they have found their own. The confusion among the lambs is greater. Mother may recognise her own youngster by the smell but her own appearance has changed so much that recognition may not be mutual. It takes some time to sort the whole business out."

Once, representatives of the brokers bargained on the spot

for the wool. Then it became customary to send bales direct to Bradford where, in the autumns of long ago, the great wool sales took place.

A dialect writer recalled a particularly lively boon clip:

> *Sek bleatin' o' lambs, and sek barkin' o' dogs,*
>   *Sek jybin' and jwokin' o' men;*
> *Sek clatt'rin' o' lads in their oald cokert clogs,*
>   *Sek drinkin' o' whisky. Amen.*

Horse Power

A horse lived on what grew on the farm and was known to "eat bare". With its weight and broad feet, it *poached* [puddled] wet ground to the extent that a Lakeland farmer reckoned he might keep three cows where he had one horse. A horse served its owner for many years with few health concerns, though an animal that had dusty food might become *brokken-winded* and have to be put down. Breaking in a horse for farm work took two or three months. The horse must become accustomed to having a bit in its mouth. It was then introduced to saddle and tracings. A common ruse was to strap a pair of old trousers, filled with straw, to a horse's back. A horse might be yoked to a log of wood to check on its capacity to pull. The blacksmith was a jack of all trades. He shod horses, being especially busy just before haytime, when it was not unusual for a queue to develop. In frosty weather he was called to remove a horse's shoes to sharpen them so the animal might keep its feet on an icy surface.

S H Cole, of Caldbeck, who took up farming locally in the 1920s, remembered when horses were used for everything except threshing. He bought a pair of Clydesdales in 1919. One horse was three years old and the other was seven. They cost 210 guineas, served him until 1939 and bred him many foals. The best horses stood between 15 and 16 h.h. Ability to handle a "swing" plough or a drill plough depended on having a pair of horses at a word and on having their willing co-oper-ation without having to bully them.

Strickland Poole, of Troutbeck, remembered when his father bought a good workhorse – maybe 10 years old – for £12. Horses were getting past their best at 20 years old, though Strickland had mown with a horse that had celebrated its 30th birthday. Tom Dixon, of Forest Hall Farm, on the eastern fells, had a white pony that he entered in a racing event at Selside. Tom would shout: "Go it frog-slother [spawn] and bent". This was an apt description of the landscape that was better known to the white pony than the lush green field in which it was running.

Each spring, from May until the end of June, an *entire* [uncastrated stallion] went the rounds, serving local mares. The attendant was not allowed to ride the animal except on the journey home. Moses Edmondson, of Ulverston, had an *entire* that was taken as far as the head of Great Langdale. Horse and attendant were in the dale once a week during the season. William Hully led an animal with the grand name of *Comet* to the same piece of ground for 20 years and the stallion served 160 mares in a season. *Comet* weighed 11 cwt but was capable of trotting a mile in three minutes.

A chap from the Whitcham Valley who visited Sawrey charged £2 a time. If it "didn't take", the farmer paid only the groom's fee. Tommy Burns operated from Wigton with one of Kilpatrick's horses. He put up at various places en route. When he took one *entire* as far as Millom, both man and horse returned by train so that they might undertake another journey on the Monday. They never travelled on a Sunday, though on that day a stallion was accommodated in a large loose-box at the *King's Head* at Bootle. A number of farmers, hearing about this, took their mares there on Sunday morning.

The Dales pony, which at 14.2 hh is somewhat larger than the fell pony, was most commonly used by packhorse owners, who moved heavy loads to and from the Lakeland communities before the transport revolution of the early nineteenth century. The fell pony was nonetheless a good pack animal. A Dales cob was sturdy, compact, short coupled [having a short back] and might carry goods weighing about 20 stone, a load being equally divided between each side. Thus laden, the cob would plod from 12 to 20 miles a day. The attendants slept rough. They carried bags of oatmeal, onions and cheese as basic foodstuffs for themselves. The ponies ate what they might find beside the track.

The tinkling from a brass bell worn by the leading horse heralded the approach of a packhorse train consisting of around 25 animals. They were interconnected, the tail of one being plaited to form a ring, through which was passed a rope that extended from the halter of the animal next in line. Ponies were shod for the long journeys. A shoe made for a pack animal had a distinctive long heel. The panniers were made of wood, connected by hinge to a bow of metal. This extended over the back of the animal. Another hinge was fitted at the point where the ledge jutted out from a pannier. Turf might be used to pad the animal's back, a disadvantage of the split-load being that it might move, giving the animal a sore back. The loads were various. Salt was in regular demand, much of the meat consumed in winter having been salted down to preserve it. Salt might be bartered against the products of the dales – against wool, cheese and butter.

Fell ponies have for long been part of the Lakeland scene, especially in the eastern areas. Some were used to do the ploughing. A Lakeland farmer described one pony as "damned near a horse, only on less legs". Fell ponies lived in a semi-wild state along the East Fellside of the northern Pennines. Groups were spread about the hills between Pooley Bridge and the head of Kentmere. Ponies crossed High Street and High Raise, where they were as much at home as sheep. Two and a-half years was the most desirable "breaking" age.

Jonty Wilson, blacksmith at Kirkby Lonsdale, was the proverbial mine of information about pack ponies. His grand-father had kept a string of animals up to the time that railways began to take over the heavy work. A load might consist of wool or cloth, lead and silver from the mines or charcoal from the pitsteads in the Furness woods. A notable old-time route, known as The Galloway Gate extended for some 130 miles from lowland Lancashire through Cumbria, via Beckfoot, near Kirkby Lonsdale, and away towards the Lune Gorge and Lyvennet valley, to an ultimate destination in south-west Scotland. Jonty took the author to the much used Scar Brow, in Lunesdale, where the passage of ponies had created a thirty foot gully.

Galloway was the name adopted for the cob that was the proverbial maid of all work on the farms. "Git in t'owd Gallowa'", a farmer might say to his son when some especially hard task had to be undertaken.

William Nuttall, whose long residence in Borrowdale began in 1887, recalled when a stable of pack ponies was kept at Dungeon Ghyll in Langdale. George Bennett, who lived there, came regularly to Borrowdale, Wasdale and Ennerdale with animals that were loaded with luggage for visitors who would be fell-walking. A stable of pack ponies kept at Wasdale Head was in charge of red-headed Joe Cunning. Within living memory, ponies and cobs were being reared on many Cumbrian farms for local use or to be sold to urban traders. A writer about Grasmere in 1875 met a man whose grandmother remembered the arrival of new bells for the church. They came over White Moss, being borne on sleds drawn by ponies. Lead needed for roofing work at Windermere church was conveyed from Whitehaven on the backs of dependable ponies.

The Gentle Shorthorn

Shorthorn cattle, introduced early in the 19th century, benefited from improvements in the condition of pasture-land. In the high dale country, they replaced a few mixed stocks of Galloways. The first task on the farm was to milk cows by hand, with the milker sitting on the traditional three-legged stool, the bucket between his or her legs. In summer, the cattle spent their days outdoors; in winter, they had the humid warmth of an outbuilding.

John Hind, a farm lad at Grange Farm in Borrowdale before the First World War, milked four cows and took a pail of milk to the farm kitchen where Mrs Coates, the farmer's wife, began the process of butter-making. To separate the cream, the milk was poured into bowls that reposed on a *benk* [shelf] in the milk-house. The shelf was formed of a slab of slate brought down from an old quarry on Castle Crag. When the milk had stood for "three meals", the cream had separated and was deftly removed using a section of a cow's horn. Cream was stored in a crock to await churning day, which on this Borrowdale farm was Thursday. The blue [skimmed] milk was fed to the young stock. Butter was retailed locally.

Rather more than fifty years ago, W Rawling, of Godferhead, a breeding farm between Loweswater and Crummock Water, concentrated on rearing Shorthorn cattle for sale. He considered that this dual purpose breed – milk and beef – was ideal for a dale-country farm. On the formation of the Northern Dairy Shorthorn Breeders' Society, all the Rawling stock was registered. At about the same time, E W Towers of Knott House Farm, Grasmere, was tenanting a hill farm at the heart of the Lake District. He retailed in the village the milk drawn from his 45 to 50 herd of cattle.

Hired Help

The heyday of the hirings was in the 19th century, when many a lad left home at the age of 14, determined to earn a living from farming. He would tramp to the nearest market town, stick a straw in his mouth and stand in the market-place – a shy, lonely lad. A dale farmer would offer him £4 for the term. If he liked the place, he might stay for two or three years, by which time he had become a competent worker. At 17, considering himself to be a man, he would return to the hirings and obtain £12 to £14 a year. He would "live in", sleep in the farmhouse and dine with the family. In better times, when he was paid £45 a year, an ambitious lad would aim to get his own dale farm.

An insight into the life of a farm labourer early in the 19th century is given by a recollection quoted by F W Garnett in his review of agriculture in Westmorland. The man had taken an empty cottage with some peat moss and a garden for half a guinea a year. His parents supplied the furniture. A local farmer engaged him for sixpence a day and his meat. He was satisfied with that plus the money his wife earned from spinning. Until he was "wedded", he worked for his father and got clothes when he needed them. He spun during winter nights. On their wedding day, he and his wife had seven shillings between them.

A century later, in 1909, a top man earned between £18 and £20 for the half year. Sturdy lads, needed on small farms, were paid between £6 and £9. In each case, board, lodgings and washing were included. The indispensable Garnett, in *Westmorland Agriculture 1800-1900*, reported that Westmorland farm labourers were superior to those of the South, both in physique and morale." Edwin Waugh (1882) wrote: "As I came away from Kendal in the train, I overheard two old farmers inquiring about the market. "Well, Jossy; hoo didta ga on aboot sarvants?" "Well, sarvant lasses is bad to hire, John. Dang it; bits o' lile lasses axin' ten pound and ten guineas... Sarvants hev nobbut two faults, John, just now: they're bad to catch – an' they're good for nowt when ye have catcht 'em."

Jack Bland, who took up residence in Kentmere in 1903, started work at Low Longmire Farm, Applethwaite, and was paid £2 for the half year. "By gum," he commented in old age, "they'd screw their noses up if they got that for a week now. Aye, they'd want it for t'day –and then they wouldn't be satis-fied, some on 'em." In 1912, when he was 13 years old, John Hind left school in Borrowdale. His school days ended when the schoolmaster said: "You can go to work. We can't do any more for you here." John became a farmer's boy at Grange Farm, the home of Jim Coates, his wife Annie and their quite young family. He began work at Martinmas (11 November), hiring for six months at £4.10s.

When the six month term was up, he was paid for his efforts, receiving sovereigns and being invited to stay on for another year, which he did, for £5. He was taught how to plough, though the field was small and devoted to growing a few potatoes for the family needs. Jim Coates had one horse and at ploughing time he borrowed another from his brother. Grange Farm being capable of providing employment for a lad, Jim was not invited to stay at the end of the year. The farmer and his lad parted amicably. John left with a good reference.

Hiring fairs took place at Whitsun and Martinmas. Men stood in a time-honoured places in the market town, where they were scrutinised by farmers. At Keswick, popular places were in the yard of the *Packhorse* inn or where farm folk were inclined to gather on a Saturday to sell butter or eggs. Around fifty young people, men and women, stood in the Top Square. A farmer wanting labour would ask for a lad's age and accom-plishments; he would seek the names of those who might testify as to his "character". (A classic story was of the lad who, when approached a second time by a farmer, and asked about his "character", declined a job with the words: "I'se got thine!"). Some of the girls could demand more than boys. They were capable of working both inside and outside a farmhouse – of doing housework and helping with the haymaking, of making butter or thinning out the turnips. Meanwhile, the lads and lasses who were unsuccessful in finding employment at Keswick prepared to go to the hirings at Cockermouth on the Monday.

A regular feature at the hiring fairs were quack doctors, offering remedies for human or animal ailments – or, indeed, for both. Among the substances peddled by these mountebanks were drops for toothache, powder to placate babies who were in a tantrum and innumerable mixtures to ward off colds and chills. It is likely that Kendal Black Drop contained laudanum. An appeal was made to Methodists via the Reverend John Wesley pills, which were perhaps intended for inner cleanliness!

When hiring fairs at Broughton and Millom dwindled, the fair at Ulverston throve as never before. Dozens of lads stood at the side of the street. If a farmer thought someone looked like "a big lump o' cheap labour", he'd go and see if he could hire him – for as little as possible. On hiring day at Kendal, it became customary for a man who wished to find a place to attach a match stalk or a piece of straw to his cap. Towards the end of the 19th century, a strong man demanded £15 for half a year's work.

At Penrith, the hirings were known as "term week". This related to the week's holiday that occurred between a farm man leaving one place on a Saturday and turning up at the next place on the following Saturday. For a few days the drudgery of farm work could be forgotten when a fair arrived in town. On being hired, a likely lad was given a shilling to fix the bargain. He was "legally fast" for a six month term at an arranged figure, which would be paid at the end of the period of service. One Borrowdale lad's first wage, at 13, was £4.10s. The largest sum he was paid, just before the onset of the First World War, was £28. By this time he could do practically every farm task. The Lakeland fell farmer did not require a specialist – the type depicted in *Mayor of Casterbridge*, the South Country novel of Thomas Hardy. In Lakeland, a man was expected to manage cattle, horses and sheep.

Being hired was chancy for both the farmer and the hired lad unless, as often happened, the recruiting farmer knew the family of one of the lads who were available. Otherwise, a lad from a poor part of town must be house-trained. Another might go to a farm where living conditions were poor and food was even worse.

John Hind had a brief holiday before, aged 13, he began work at Grange Farm, Borrowdale, at Martinmas. Tommy Graham, the Keswick carter, transported him and his tin trunk to the farm. John was wearing an old jacket, a shirt made by his mother – the shirt fastened at the back – and corduroy trousers ordered from Mr Huggins, the "bag man", who lived at Ambleside. He wore clogs, made by Ernie Plaskett of Rosthwaite.

The farmer set him to work helping to milk forty cows twice a day. He was roused from his bed at 4 a.m., for the milk must be available for sale by 7 a.m. The lad's sleeping quarters were in a tiny space over the kitchen to which access was by ladder. So constricted was the space beneath the slanting roof he couldn't open his trunk unless he slid it towards his metal-framed bed. He slept on a feather mattress, though some hired men were provided with a *caff* [chaff] bed. The mattress had been stuffed with left-overs on threshing days.

Most hired lads settled affably into farmhouse life and invariably joined the family for meals. On winter evenings, they shared space at the fireside with the family. Dickinson, in *Cumbriana*, wrote:

O' fare alike, beath measter and man,
In eatin' and drinkin' and wark;
They turned out at morning and togidder began
And left off togidder at night.

Girls fresh from school, hired for work at the farms, strove long and hard to maintain an exacting domestic routine.

A servant girl at High Lodore rose early from her bed and washed in an outside trough. A farmer's wife shouted to her servant girl, who had just got out of bed, "What's ta dewin', Laura?" "Oh – I'se fastening me brat [apron]." "Nay – fasten it when thou's coming downstairs – and lowse it when thou's goin' to bed." Water had to be carried from the beck or the hand pump in the yard. On wash-day, the stone copper was filled, bucket by bucket, and boiled for the family wash. One spat on a flat iron to assess the heat. Each day, there were lamps to be filled, lamp-glasses to be cleaned and candles to be placed in the bedrooms. The wooden kitchen table must be scoured with fine sand.

After the First World War, when there was considerable unemployment in industrial centres like Barrow-in-Furness, life on a farm was preferable to poverty. It was enough for a lad to have a place where he might eat and sleep. At Ulverston, a farmer hired an out-of-work man with a "pinched face" who said he would work for nothing if he could find a place where he could have regular food and be warm. He had almost starved to death in the previous winter. The new environment might be wild and strange but meals were regular and wholesome. The farmer's wife, brought up to be clean and tidy, was sometimes aghast at the dirty condition of the new arrival. After repeated complaints to a dirty lad, the farmer took him in hand, put him in a bath and scrubbed away the caked layers of grime.

If the hired lad was part of the overspill of a large farming family, he would need little introduction to farm work. The town lad was on a steep learning curve. He was taught how to milk and how to "muck out" the shippons, emptying a muck midden and following a traditional routine when spreading the muck to enliven jaded meadows. With several miles of drystone wall on the farm, he would also be taught how to gap-wall, reinstating a section that had collapsed. The primary concern was the welfare of the stock. The hired man worked long days at lambing time or when the sheep were being dipped or shorn.

The prospects for an ambitious lad were good. He might become a farm manager or acquire the tenancy of a small-holding, with the object of moving to larger farms in coming years. Some young men, unable to rent a small farm, emigrated to Canada or Australia. For a bachelor who had not saved for his old age, life became especially hard. He would work until he died, "fair-mashed up".

Outhgill

Food for the Home

OS Macdonell, in *George Ashbury*, a novel of olden days, wrote of a Lakeland farmhouse: "There was a small room used as a scullery, and beyond this was a door through which they went into the kitchen-living-room. It was a fair-sized place; there was a large open fire-place in which burned a big fire of peat and wood. On the fire were a number of good-sized cooking pots, which gave out a very pleasant smell of food. An oaken table stood in the middle of the room and on it was a coarse but clean linen cloth. There were only two chairs used by the parents; the others sat upon a settle and on small stools."

Daniel Scott (1899) wrote that in country cottages and farm houses, the chimneys had no flues. They were funnel-shaped – very wide at the bottom, contracting to the top, where the aperture was the size of an ordinary chimney, through which the smoke escaped. "In these open chimneys hams, legs of beef, flitches of bacon and whole carcasses of mutton were hung to dry for winter consumption." Fowls running round the farm-yard were fed with some corn and mash produced in an outside boiler. Money from the sale of eggs was the housewife's only source of independent income.

In most cases, food at Lakeland farms was good, being plentiful and wholesome. Breakfast consisted of poddish [porridge], home-cured ham, home-laid eggs and home-baked bread. Bread and a dollop of cheese were available for "elevenses". For dinner, meat and vegetables were consumed. An early tea was followed by supper at about 6 p.m. Crowdy was, according to Daniel Scott, "an excellent and invigorating species of soup, made by pouring the liquor in which beef was boiling over oatmeal in a basin. Oatmeal also entered into the composition of pie-crusts and gingerbread as, for example, with Kendal *piggin bottoms* – snaps, stamped out of rolled dough by the iron rim that formed the external base of the wooden *piggin* or *biggin* [a small wooden tub].

Every farm kept one or two pigs. William Middlesbrough, who had a small farm Newbiggin, was rarely there during pig-killing time. His two sons did the work while he was touring on ponyback slaughtering about five pigs a day. A fell farmer was charged half a crown a pig. If a farmer wished him to return the next day to cut up the carcass, a further shilling was exacted. Geese were killed and plucked for sale just before Christmas. It was often after midnight before the pluckers went to their beds. Next day the "dirty work" started. The bodies were scalded and trussed. Goose blood was saved and groats added to make black puddings. Goose grease was rubbed on the chests of ailing children or smeared on boots to make them waterproof.

Scarcely anything of the domestic goose was wasted. Goose giblets, washed and cut into uniform sized pieces and mixed with half a pound of stewing steak, were transformed into a tasty pie. The mixture, seasoned with salt and pepper, and given a dash a thyme and parsley, was stewed gently for several hours before being placed in a pie dish, with a short crust, and baked until brown. Tatie pot was, to the Lakelander, what haggis is to the Scotsman. The neck and loin chops of mutton, neatly trimmed, were placed in an earthenware jar and partly cooked in the oven. The meat was then overspread with a layer of peeled potatoes and chopped onions. This was roasted until the top potatoes were well browned.

Every housewife made her own bread. Rum butter, served on special occasions, like christenings, was a mixture of rum, sugar and nutmeg. It was dispensed to nursing mothers in the confident hope that it would help them to recover from their confinement. A Cartmel recipe was to melt together half a pound of butter and one pound of soft brown sugar. They must not be allowed to boil. A little grated nutmeg was added before the mixture was beaten up well. It was time to add a table-spoon of rum. As it began to cool, the rum butter was placed in a dish or basin. It was usually served on crackers.

Gingerbread, made of butter, brown sugar and golden syrup, was left to cool for a short time, cut into fingers, placed on a wire tray to cool and then stored in an airtight tin. Westmorland Farmhouse Pie was made of fresh beef, mutton, rashers of lean bacon or ham, along with onions, carrot, pota-toes, then dashed with pepper and salt. Herb pudding was made in spring when the "patience dock" was still in leaf. This plant, also known as the Passion dock or Easter-ledge, grew in damp hollows and produced delicate pink bottlebrush flowers. The leaves were cut small, mixed with barley, young nettles and other tender green leaves, also an egg, well-beaten. The whole was boiled in a pudding cloth.

Duddon Valley

A Sporting Life

In nearly all the parishes, churchwarden's accounts contained references to payments made for the heads of foxes. Such money was paid out at regular intervals. The wardens did not worry if the money found its way to local inns. This early idea of a fox fund was popular. A dead fox was a pleasant sight to a sheep farmer. In the parish of Crosthwaite, the wardens paid ten shillings for a fox head. At Greystoke, the figure was 3s.4d, representing ten quarts of ale. It was the custom for a farmer to keep a hound or two for hare coursing or fox-hunting. After a service, a churchwarden would mount a tombstone and tell of forthcoming hunts, sales and auctions that were to take place during the coming week. Eventually, packs of hounds were kept and the sport was ritualised.

In the old days fell foxes were less plentiful than they are now. Richard Clapham, whose interest in hunting led him to study them carefully, was asked what was their favourite food. He replied: "Beetles". Hundreds of black beetles crawled on the sheep-trods. There was a profusion of wing cases in the droppings of foxes. When Joe Bowman was huntsman of the Ullswater pack, the number of foxes killed in a hunting season would be between seven or eight brace. The old fell fox was considered to be a markedly different type from the Midland strain. Known as "greyhound foxes" the fell type were long in the leg, their coat being sprinkled with silvery hairs. The longest fox that the Ullswater killed measured five feet from the tip of its nose to the end of its brush. It weighed 18½ lb, compared with an average of 15 lb in the lowlands.

The craggy nature of the Lakeland fells was an antithesis of the average hunting country. The fell hounds were for the most part light-coloured, white predominating, so they might be seen against a generally dark background. A good hound should *throw his tongue* [give voice lustily] when running or marking a fox in one of the *borrans* [rock-earths]. The huntsman, being on foot, usually had only their cries to go by. The hounds were mustered in spring if a fox was known to be worrying lambs. Meets were early, before the sun dispelled the dew and spoiled the scent.

Hound-trailing as a sport has figured in local histories since the 18th century. Trailing was recorded at Flan Sports, Ulverston, in 1836 and at Langholm Gala in 1840. Hounds taking part in these events were from the packs kept for fox-hunting. It is possible that hounds first hunted fox skin. A trail hound seems a mournful animal. Its slim, lean body is draped by loose skin. The hound looks half-starved but, in fact, eats better than its owner. One man fed his hound on whites of egg – considering that the yolk was not good for them – and glucose. He thought nothing of visiting a butcher's shop for two or three pounds of shin beef.

Betting takes place. It does not stop when a race has begun. Men known as "blowers", travelling in cars, studied form while the hounds were still running. Years ago, walkie-talkie sets were used to communicate with the showfield. Rockets were let off to pass on information to the field. The scent laid usually takes the form of aniseed, diluted with paraffin and with turpentine to lift the scent so a hound would not wear out its nose on the ground. Rags are soaked, then dragged round the course. Meeting half-way round the course, the trailers work exactly. A hound trail is void if it lasts for less than 25 minutes or over 45 minutes. One of the trail men advances on the field where the excited hounds and equally excited owners await.

When wrestling was enjoying its greatest popularity, competitions took place in almost every village. This was an inexpensive sport. Among its exponents were hired lads from the dale farms who, earning £6 to £8 and "keep" for six months hard labour on dale farms, had to subsist on little more than bare hands and empty pockets. A cheap way of passing an evening was to turn up at a village green and *tak 'od*, Cumberland and Westmorland style, which demanded brains as well as brawn. Meanwhile, on the farm, a padded post might be used to perfect the classic *holds* and *chips*. Wind and stamina were improved by hauling a farm cart about a field.

The Lakeland type of wrestling is not a matter of brute force. As a competitor whirls himself and his opponent, you see the solution of many complicated problems of stresses and strains, twists and levers and instinctive moves. A bellman summons wrestlers or, if they do not appear for their bouts, "blows them out". A friendly sport, taking place in a "ring" formed by two judges and a referee, the wrestling begins when the combatants shake hands. Then each man places his chin on his opponent's right shoulder and grasps him round the back, the left arm of one wrestler lying over the opponent's right and the right arm under the other's left arm. The style, sometimes known as *back hold* wrestling, seems complicated when described but looks easy and natural. If a wrestler breaks hold before the other had been floored he loses the bout.

The traditional costume of white "long johns", vest and embroidered velvet trunks dates back to Victorian times. The visual impact led to prizes being awarded for the neatest costumes and womenfolk spent long hours in decorative needlework. The designs grew more ornate with the passing of time. When the Cumberland and Westmorland Wresting Association met in 2005, it was decided to deregulate the dress code for championship events. Competitors would no longer be required to wear the traditional garb, an attempt to stop youngsters from drifting out of the sport. They would be allowed to wrestle in something comfortable. Football shirts and tracksuits were now in order.

The officials, kneeling on mats, a low vantage point, keep a sharp eye every move. In putting his opponent on the ground, a wrestler might choose one of seven or eight different *chips*, the most celebrated being the *cross buttock*. In this neat move, a wrestler puts his buttock quickly under the other man's stomach, which he uses as a fulcrum, throwing him over his head or shoulder. If it doesn't succeed, the wrestler who tried it finds himself vulnerable to being thrown. Wrestlers of old told the story of Hugh Hird of Troutbeck who, visiting London, wrestled (and defeated) the king's champion. Hugh described his diet as "thick poddish that a mouse might walk on dry-shod for breakfast and the sunny side of a *wether* [sheep] for dinner." The story is apocryphal, but who needs such tales for a local type of wrestling that threw up legends galore?

The "big names" at Grasmere Sports were Gilpin Bland, Joe Noble, Steve and Wilson Knowles and Billy Kirkby. Charles Dickens, visiting the Lakes in 1857, watched William Richardson win his 175th belt. George Sreadman, champion of champions, stood close on 6 ft tall, weighed 18 stone and had a chest measurement of 52 in. This remarkable man wrestled in public from 1865 until 1900. He dominated the heavy-weight classes at Grasmere for thirty years. Another six-footer, Tom Longmire, was hailed as "the hero of a hundred rings". Tom was in action for 20 years, winning over 170 belts.

Smuggling

Lakeland had its distillers and distributors of whisky. They used a kettle with a contrivance known as a *worm* – equipment that was easily assembled, quickly dismantled and might be hidden away among rocks. Bog water helped to flavour the liquid. Among the dalesfolk who ignored the Distillery Act of 1834 was Lanty Slee, who distilled whisky in tucked-away places on the hills above Little Langdale, without the knowledge of the Revenue authorities.

Lanty's best whisky was transported in bottles and bladders to the gentry at 10s a gallon. It is said that when moving whisky by pony, the feet of pony were bound with straw and the smugglers wore sacking on their shoes. He was caught in 1853. His still was confiscated. Lanty appeared protestingly before the bench at Hawkshead, some of whom would have been regularly supplied by Lanty on making an innocent inquiry: "Have you had a good crop of taties this year?" He made, from potato peelings, a potent spirit that must be watered down 50 per cent before being drunk.

Apart from secluded fellside hidey-holes, Lanty hid a still beneath the flags of his kitchen at Low Arnside farm. A long pipe carried the exhaust steam from the house into a hedge in an adjoining field. Another improvised distillery was tucked away among birch trees in Atkinson Coppice. This site was reached by swinging down a hole among the rocks on a rope. After his last conviction he became "respectable" – though not respectable enough to prevent him from having a crude distillery near the shore of Red Tarn, a mile above the Three Shires stone and almost 2,000 ft above sea level. Perhaps the whisky he produced here was just for his friends.

At Wasdale Head stood a farm called Row Foot, the home of Will Ritson since his birth in 1808. Will, farmer cum innkeeper, had obtained an excise licence to sell liquor in 1856. In previous years, he had dealt with much smuggled liquor, brought quietly inland from Ravenglass. Revenue officers who followed that trail surreptitiously were not keen to enter the fastnesses of Wasdale. Will retired to Nether Wasdale in 1879 and died there in 1890.

Smugglers deposited kegs of the "hard stuff" in the crypt of Whitbeck Chapel, which stood at the foot of Black Combe, not far from the shore. It was said that among the verses sung by the congregation was:

> *There's a Spirit above, and a spirit below;*
> *A Spirit of love and a spirit of woe.*
> *The Spirit above is the Spirit Divine.*
> *But the spirit below is the spirit of wine.*

Changeful Days

Fifty years ago, Isaac Myers of Great Langdale forecast that the time was not far distant when the dales would be playgrounds and farming just a memory. Farmhouses would become tea houses and meadows filled with caravans and tents. The Lake District National Park and The National Trust ensure there is no dramatic change to buildings or land use but dale-country life has changed in more subtle ways. Farms have been amalgamated to form more economic units. New ways of keeping and feeding cattle mean that outbuildings and outbarns, having become redundant, are converted into dwellings at a cost far above what a local couple could afford. There have been doleful prophecies of the demise of hill farming.

Lakeland life was transformed from 1847, when a railway was constructed to the hamlet of Applethwaite, near Windermere. The railway company adopted the name Windermere and this was also used by the town that evolved at the railhead. Keswick was eventually linked with the rail network. It saw the start of tourism and the dilution of dale life as it had been known for centuries. Into the herdwick country, within living memory, came a breed of sheep called the Swaledale. Quick and bright eyes stared out from a head that was dark complexioned on the upper part, grey or mealy lower down. Strong horns curled round low on either side. A sturdy body was clothed tightly and thickly with white wool.

The type had been fixed and bred to by farmers living on and around Tan Hill, on the Yorkshire-Westmorland border. Its spread across the north-country began in the 1920s, with the formation of a breed society. The Swaledale, more at home on peaty ground than the rocky areas where the herdwick thrives, was nonetheless more profitable. The herdwick has survived, mainly through the efforts of Beatrix Potter, author of popular children's books, and The National Trust. Miss Potter (who became Mrs Heelis) lived at Near Sawrey but bought up many dalehead farms, which she bequeathed to the Trust, one condition being that the herdwick should continue to be kept there.

Harry Tyson, reflecting on his life in Wasdale from the death of his father in 1953, mentioned the hard times the fell farmers experienced in the 1920s and 1930s. Milk production had become a good standby now that he was sure of a market. He and his two sons, John and Ernest, were milking 10 or 11 out of 30 beasts. They were mainly Shorthorn, which did well on rough grazings. Old farmers were against artificial fertilisers but he considered they were valuable if used properly. He was applying basic slag, some lime and North African phosphates. In the old days, everything had to be carried by horse and cart from the railway station at Seascale. One load represented a day's work. Now he was ordering it and it was being delivered to the farm. The same applied to coal. Half a ton of coal lasted a long time. Up to the mid-1940s they burnt a lot of peat, which they cut, dried and carted locally. He was still using horses, considering that tractors would be of little use. But generally horses were disappearing from the countryside. There was also a sharp decline in the human population. Labour was hard to get. Lack of amenities and a bus service deterred many young people.

In the early 1950s, Mary Fair of Holmrook was lamenting the decline in dialect. She was also observing that the romantics who thronged our dales in the nineteenth century foisted mongrel place-names upon us – ghyll for hill, Scawfell for Scafell and Saddleback for Blencathra.

Grizedale Forest, now a major tourist attraction as well as a commercial enterprise, has a history that spans centuries. Its name evokes its Norse past, when it was "the valley where young pigs were kept". From the 11th century, the Cistercian monks of Furness Abbey were active here, clearing broadleafed wood in order to provide pastures for sheep, the sale of the wool from which was a major source of income. Other areas were coppiced, providing timber, firewood and charcoal.

In the 18th century, Agnes Ford inherited the estate. She returned the area to its old woodland state. In the 1780s, she arranged for the planting of over 70,000 oak and other broadleaved trees. More trees were planted when Agnes had married Henry Ainslie. This time, the accent was upon softwoods, larch mainly, which Wordsworth described as "vegetable manufactory". When Montague Ainslie inherited the estate early in the 19th century, a further one and a-half million larch trees were introduced. Now that the sale of softwoods was remunerative, the accent was upon conifers. Harold Brocklebank took over Grizedale estate in 1903. Forest management continued to be a prime activity, giving his new hall a forest setting.

During the 1939-45 war, plantations were felled to provide scarce essentials such as pit props. The hall became part of a prisoner of war camp. One of the German prisoners, Hans von Werra, a Luftwaffe ace, achieved widespread fame when he managed to escape. The forestry tradition was continued and expanded by the Forestry Commission. Grizedale Forest is now a centre for diverse outdoor activity, including waymarked trails, beside which are specially commissioned sculptures reflecting the forest culture.

The National Trust, owners of many a fine dalehead sheep farm in Lakeland, in a policy statement issued in the early 1960s, acknowledge that much of the character of the district depended upon its farming, both as regards the detail round about the farmstead and in general on the fells and in the fields. "Unless both the tenant-farmer and his landlord are prosperous there is no hope of keeping the house and buildings in trim repair let alone carrying out necessary improvements in the traditional local style, nor will the right type of tenant be attracted when the farms come to be re-let. Upon the right type of tenant and his prosperity depends the continuation of the characteristic way of farming based mainly on fell-sheep and stock rearing. It is said that fell farming is not so much an industry but more of a way of life; certainly the man who can put up stone walls and knows how to manage sheep among the fells needs to have been born and bred amongst them..."

In a report issued by C H D Acland, the Trust's Regional Agent, in 1972, it was stated that the Trust has always known that the fell farmer plays a large part in the preservation of the Lake District scene. Because of this it has built up its farms so that the tenants can produce a fair living from agriculture. This process consists partly of increasing the size of the holdings. Another aspect was bringing the fixed equipment of each farm up to a standard that would enable the tenant to achieve full and economic production; so the design of new farm buildings, and the repair of old ones, is done so unobtrusively as to go almost unnoticed.

In 2005, carpets were being made in Kendal using the herd-wick wool-clip from 140 fell farms. The scheme, a partnership between Goodacres and the National Trust, led to Goodacre's herdwick carpets bearing the Trust logo and brand. A licence fee was being paid to the Trust, the fee being passed to farmers for their fleeces. Three years before, wool was routinely burned, being worthy barely 2p a fleece. A drop in the price paid for fleeces meant that 50p a fleece was being offered, which was about 10p less than the cost of clipping a sheep – but, as one or two farmers wrly observed, was a lot better than nothing. The heavyweight and densely-constructed carpets were being made available in a range of rustic hues.

An impetus to keep the drystone walls in good order came in 1968 with the founding of the Dry Stone Walling Association of Great Britain. There had been a period of decline. Competitions were held throughout the country. Anyone who took part was given a day to rebuild two metres of a dilapidated stone wall. A tonne of stone is needed to make two metres of wall. A good waller might construct from three to four metres of wall a day, his progress depending on the size and nature of the available stone. Recent efforts to rejuvenate the upland vegetation are bearing fruit. With less intensive grazing than during and after the 1930-45 war, heather and bilberry, with their attendant flowers, butterflies and bees, are growing back. Lowland fields similarly show a recovery, especially where grants have been available to avoid over-use.

In Cumbria, the decrease in the number of cattle and sheep has been especially marked since a serious outbreak of foot and mouth disease led to a massive cull of stock, from which – thankfully – most of the herdwick sheep were spared. A report by a member of the staff of the Cumbria Wildlife Trust concludes: "However, it may be that we shall reach a point where there will not be enough grazing animals to maintain valuable open space habitats. It may therefore be that heavy grazing of the fells, which has been one of the Trust's key concerns over the past forty years, will disappear to be replaced by the need to ensure that some areas remain grazed at all."

The Lakeland farmers of the future will be matching their efforts to global warming. Sir Ben Hill, the former head of the National Farmers' Union, told a Penrith conference on farming futures, held in February, 2005, that the region could do "pretty well" in a warmed-up world. As long as the Gulf Stream remained, North West England would retain a climate suitable for livestock rearing on grassland and for growing increasingly important fuel crops. Fossil fuels would have to be replaced and this can be done from the land. Increased cheese-making and a larger share of the lamb market were also in prospect.

In March, 2005, four years after parts of Cumbria had been ravaged by foot and mouth disease, the painstaking task of putting the territorial instinct back into a fell flock entered a new phase. Tony Temple, of Black Hall Farm, near Cockley Beck, at the head of the Duddon Valley, delivered the fourth generation of lambs born since the 2001 outbreak. It was the half-way point in an experiment to re-heft his new 1,000 flock of herdwicks using electric fences. He lost almost his entire flock – at a 800-year-old farmstead.

Tony built up another flock. About 300 of his young stock avoided the disease because at the time it struck they were wintering on low land away from the farm. The number was augmented by purchases. To keep the incoming sheep from straying, he erected seven miles of electric fencing, orange in hue, in a temporary basis. Hopefully, seven or eight generations down the line, his flock would have learned to stay on the farm. There was a fixed time by which the fencing had to be removed.

Thus does the hardy little herdwick sheep maintain a position in the Lake District it has occupied since prehistory. The wool is coarse but its flesh is the mutton of kings – or queens. In 1953, it was served at the Coronation banquet of Queen Elizabeth II. Herdwick mutton was on the menu when she visited the old sheep farm of High Yewdale, near Coniston.

The Countryside and Rights of Way Act, which became effective in May, 2005, mean that the public might walk freely over about 500 square miles, rather more than half of the National Park. The Ordnance Survey brought out a range of new maps, showing areas of land that had just been opened to the walker.

In 2005, the Lake District National Park and North West Development Agency began a process by which the prized World Heritage status for Lakeland might be attained. The state of Lakeland today, both physically and culturally, has been created largely by the unnumbered generations of Lakeland farmfolk, since the time – 5,000 years ago – when people entered a wilderness and set about taming it.

Bibliography

Baldwin, John R and Whyte, Ian D, *The Scandinavians in Cumbria* (1985)

Bailey, Richard N, *Viking Age Sculpture in Northern England* (1980)

Barber, Samuel, *Beneath Helvellyn's Shade* (1892)

Brunskill, R W, *Vernacular Architecture of the Lake Counties* (1974); *Traditional Farm Buildings of Britain* (1987)

Collingwood, W G, *Lake District History* (1925)

Cumbria magazine (various issues)

Darby, H C, *Geographical Magazine* (vol 126)

Hinchliffe, Isaac, *A Backwater in Lakeland* (1925)

Macdonell, O S, *Thorston Hall* (c1930)

Marshall, J D, *"Statesmen" in Cumbria. Transactions of C&W A&A Soc* (Vol LXXII, 1972)

Martineau, Harriet, *A Complete Guide to the English Lakes* (1855)

Millward, Roy, and Robinson, Adrian, *The Lake District* (1970)

Mitchell, W R, *Men of Lakeland* (1966), *Wild Cumbria* (1978), *Lakeland Dalesfolk* (1983), *Changing Lakeland* (1989), *How They Lived in the Lake District* (2002)

Nicholson, Norman, *Portrait of the Lakes* (1963)

Northern Counties Magazine, The (July, 1901)

Otley, Jonathan, *The English Lakes and Adjacent Mountains* (1834)

Page, Jim Taylor, *A Field Guide to the Lake District* (1984)

Palmer, J H, *Historic Farmhouses in and around Westmorland* (1952)

Palmer, William T, *Byways in Lakeland* (1952)

Pearsall, W H, and Pennington, W, *The Lake District* (1973)

Price, Nancy, *Shadows on the Hills* (1935)

Robinson, John, *A Guide to the Lakes* (1819)

Rollinson, William, *A History of Man in the Lake District* (1967), *A History of Cumberland and Westmorland* (1978), *A Cumbrian Dictionary* (1997)

Scott, Daniel, *Bygone Cumberland and Westmorland* (1899)

Slack, Margaret, *Lakeland Discovered* (1982)

Swift, Jeff, *Over the Gate, Westmorland Gazette* (2005)

Taylor, Christopher D., *Portrait of Windermere* (1983)

Thompson, B L, *Prose of Lakeland* (1954)

Waugh, Edwin, *Rambles in the Lake Country* (1882)

Widdup, Henry L, *Christianity in Cumbria* (1981)

If you have enjoyed this book,
you will enjoy...

KESWICK AND
NORTHERN LAKELAND

by W R Mitchell and R G K Gudgeon

Informative, practical and well-illustrated, with many pictures in colour, the book deals with landscape, history, wildlife and flora, plus twenty detailed walks in a delectable area.

A DalesCountry Book. £8.95.

VILLAGES OF THE LAKE DISTRICT

by W R Mitchell

A video production, also available in DVD, this tour of Lakeland villages combines outstanding photography, informative narration, delivered in situ, music carefully chosen to delight without being too obtrusive.

55 minutes. A Kingfisher Production. £12.95.

From: The Dalesmade Centre, Watershed Mill, Settle, North Yorkshire.

DalesCountry